Twisted
Knickers
&
Stolen
Scones

Twisted
Knickers
&
Stolen
Scones

Watt Nicoll

Lindsay Publications

First published in 1998 by
Lindsay Publications
Glasgow

© Watt Nicoll 1998

British Library Cataloguing-in-Publication Data
A Catalogue record for this book is available
from the British Library

ISBN 1 898169 15 2

Designed and typeset by Mitchell Graphics, Glasgow

Printed and bound by Bell & Bain, Limited, Glasgow

Watt Nicoll – Folk singer, piper, TV personality, scriptwriter, speedway rider, husband (persistent) and father – the list is endless and probably best summed up as *Twentieth Century Rennaissance Man in a Bright Bow Tie*! A personality as warming as the summer sun with a vitality and love of life and fellow mankind which lightens the load of companions and declares out loud that life is FUN.

In today's world of management jargon he is an acknowledged expert in "Personal Development" and "Motivation" which he calls, "Taking responsibility for your own actions". He has done much to help many, at all levels from the high achievers to those struggling to find their place in a seemingly harsh world and by his own enthusiasm and joy still shouts to the world that life is exciting, that time is precious and that every moment is to be lived to the full.

TLM SUNTER,
Executive Director, Institute of Directors

ACKNOWLEDGEMENTS

I don't believe there is such a thing as extraordinary people but there are ordinary people who are prepared to do something extra and many of them are mentioned in this book.

I would like to acknowledge their inspiration, advice and example as well as that of Bob Adams, Allison Brannan, Owen McGhee, Anita Cain, Gordon Lee, Gary McEwan, David Munro, Fiona Gibb, Carolyn Mankowitz, Jackie Hall, Jackie Osei Tutu, Elaine Reilly, Marie Leslie and thousands of others who have helped me become someone I am happy to be.

You possibly don't know some of these people and that is, unfortunately, your loss. I know them and am the better for it.

Dedication

The book is dedicated to my mother and father who loved me enough to encourage me to stand up and have the strength to walk away from them and to take the responsibility for my own decisions.

Maybe, just maybe, a wee bit of them shines through and that is why I am the best at what I do. My father always told me, "If you want to be the best you have to be better than just good."

CONTENTS

It isn't enough to know the words
It isn't enough to know the tune
You have to learn the song

Why are you reading this book ?

O F ALL THE BOOKS in all the bookshops in all the towns and cities throughout the world, whatever has possessed you to invest some of your precious life time in reading this particular book? What do you hope to gain from reading it?

This may seem like a strange question from the author, who you probably feel should be grateful for your interest, but the essential purpose of writing the book is my endeavour to **clarify thinking and establish purpose** and, if you haven't thought about it, **there is no purpose in continuing to read**.

Let me give you some immediate advice. What you read most definitely has an effect on how you think. You are feeding pieces of information into your memory and they will not go away of their own accord but rather involve other thought processes and misrepresent your intellect and ability to generate original thoughts. I truly believe, for instance, the first step for anyone embarking on a self development campaign is to choose a daily newspaper that reports facts and leaves the reader to form a personal opinion as opposed to a sensation sheet that implies editorial opinion is historic fact and grants the reader no capacity or license to think for themselves.

So! Are you reading this book because your employer has obligated you or because a friend has embarrassed you by giving it as a gift? Perhaps you were attracted to the title and are disappointed that there are no accompanying pictures or illustrations.

If you have selected this book from all the other personal development material available on the bookshelves because you were attracted to the vision of knickers in disarray then you have a natural advantage over the majority in the pursuit of personal motivation .

You know what turns you on!

Knowing what you want and why you want it is at the very heart of success. Understanding why you do anything from scratching your bum to baking a cake is the basic driving force behind genuine effort and the missing ingredient in the lethargic, indifferent attitude of the majority of today's Western society. So, before you get your knickers in a twist, let me ask you again.

Why are you reading this book?

Could it be that you were simply bored and this was the only reading material available to you or, on the other hand, could it be that you have had the book enthusiastically recommended and now eagerly anticipate a rewarding, entertaining or educational experience? Perhaps you have heard me speak at some event or have attended a seminar or workshop and think you might pick up a few good anecdotes for your own presentations.

The important factor here is that 'Twisted Knickers' embraces the practises that it preaches and that we must establish why you have decided to read it.

Once you know **'why'** you want to do something you create an expectancy and you can establish **'how'** to do it. In this instance, if you know why you are reading the book, you instantly know how to read it.

If you are looking for a story-line, a wee bash of human drama, or some embarrassments recounted and feel you can relate to life experiences, skip over the personal development technique exercises. (They are only for those who want to improve their quality of life).

Those of you who genuinely recognise that if you do what you have always done you will get what you have always got and have decided to toss that lot in the bin and go for a higher plateau will want to get down to the life changing applications. Locate them and save yourself some valuable time.

If you merely want a few quotable lines or a couple of good anecdotal tales try pages 28, 44, 52, 66 and 155 and remember to quote the name of Watt Nicoll MP every time you use them or forever live in fear of your parentage being publicly challenged.

In every instance, in every area of every facet of life, it is essential to establish what you expect, to know your desired outcome from any activity and therefor be in a position to measure the intensity of your participation.

In all the workshops and seminars I conduct, anywhere in the world, I start by establishing what those attending expect to gain from their participation and it never fails to astound me that very few people know what to expect and have not really considered fully what they want from the event.

The natural follow through is to then establish what they expect from their life, and the sad truth is that I meet very few people who know what they want. I do meet a majority who think they know what they want but **there is a world of difference between knowing what you want and thinking you know what you want.** Let me clarify this.

When pressed, I find the majority of people want one of two things – MONEY or, and I can see some nice wee woman shaking her head now as I parade number two favourite in the 'WHAT I WANT OUT OF LIFE' league.

I am constantly confronted by nice wee wifies and wee fat banal men who tell me, almost with sympathy for everyone they perceive to be mercenary, that they are not motivated by money and only want to be HAPPY.

Let me say that I have no problem with either. Our society is structured in such a way that we need money to buy peace of mind, to pay our bills and generally participate in society. I've had money and I've been boracic and I've got to say that having it is a one hundred percent improvement on not having it. I can equally and honestly also associate with those who just want to be happy.

I would, however, insist that the 'Happy Chappies' have to peel a skin off their onion and enquire into what it would take to make them happy and I would further suggest that, whilst the positive ingredient could be as varied as there are individuals in the world, the one thing that would not make them happy is to be without money.

Mrs Wumman regularly accosts me with statements like:

"I have never been motivated by money and never will be. I just want a nice home for my children and I just want to be there for them when life throws them a wee wobbly. I just want to be able to support them in any career they decide to follow"

"That is absolutely wonderful Mrs.Wumman, but tell me what do you think it would take to do all that"?

"A mothers' love and – and – and – maybe a little money"

"Exactly Mrs.Wumman, it would take money, so we now have a common starting point. We are all agreed that we want money".

Now you might start understanding the importance of knowing why you are reading this book, or any other book, or indeed why you do anything. If you just do something without purpose or expectancy then it will be meaningless. If you know what you want from any activity then you know why you are doing it and that 'purpose' will become something you expect to achieve. When you expect something you mentally prepare for it and it is that mindset that motivates you.

A telephone directory is a magnificent feat of publishing skill but could you imagine anything more meaningless than reading a telephone directory for the story line. Unless you are looking for a particular name or number and there is a purpose to you finding this information and, you therefor know what you want from the reading and why you want it and expect to find it, I cannot imagine too many placing the BT yellow pages at the top of their preferred reading list.

So **if you know why you are reading this book** and what you want from it, you will expect to find this something within its' pages and you will search for it and, because you have mentally prepared for it, **you will find what you want**. I guarantee it!

Personal experience leads me to believe that quality thinking can lift the most incapable of people to the comparative dizzy heights of social competence and provide the 'capable' with a mindset that will motivate them to maximise their personal potential and become everything they are capable of being.

At regular intervals throughout the book I will ask you to evaluate the benefits of the previous section and might even ask you to re-evaluate some sections.

This is a focus technique and is one you can employ in any learning situation.

Break down the big picture into understandable chunks and decide whether that information is fully understood, relevant to you, useful to you and, if so, where and how you would use it.

Try Evaluating what you have read so far:

- Do you understand the intended purpose of the previous chapter?
- Was the purpose achieved?
- Was the message relevant to you?
- Can you use this information?
- Will you use this information?
- How will you use this information?
- Where and when will you use it?

Dependent on how far down that list you answered positively you should now choose from the following:

- Progress to the next stage
- Read the previous chapter again
- Chuck the book in the bin

Thinking is recognised as being one of the most tiring activities known to man
Which probably accounts for so few doing much of it for themselves.

Introduction to Watt Nicoll MP

IN MY ADULT LIFE I set out to be a vet, studied zoology, rode on the professional speedway, apprenticed as a saw doctor, recorded fourteen albums as a folk singer, worked as a script writer, playwright, window cleaner, stage hypnotist, dustman and television presenter. I've spent long periods in hospital, married, divorced, travelled abroad, become well off, remarried, become bankrupt and slept rough. I have also had considerable experience as a son, a father, a husband and a friend.

I was born in Dundee on Christmas Eve 1935, the only child of a Dundee timber craftsman and an Aberdonian dressmaker. We lived in a room and kitchen in a tenement flat with toilet on the landing, which we shared with the neighbours who lived opposite. Many would see this as a disadvantaged start in life, but I was happy from day one. Tenement dwellers were the traditional progression from the Scottish clans and the fore runners to the hippie communes of the sixties. We had sixteen wee houses up our stair and that meant that every child who lived in that tenement had sixteen mummies and sixteen daddies. Truth to tell I think for many kids it was sixteen mammies and thirty two daddies because there was a great deal of shift work in these days.

I can remember not only the names, but intricate details of those I knew only in passing at that time, often with much more clarity than those I have had meaningful relationships with since, and although I have many memories of infancy, first day at school and suchlike, I most vividly recall wanting to play the bagpipes more than anything else in the world.

By the time I was five I could play the practice chanter well enough but had to be content for another three years until my parents could afford a full set of bagpipes and I reached that higher plain where fellow beings congregate to applaud you.

I initially accompanied highland dancers whilst being sought after by most of the pipe bands in Dundee and I enjoyed having identity. I was Nicoll the Boy Piper and no longer just Chic Nicoll's laddie. Throughout all the Highland Games and piping competitions, the variety shows and the press coverage of these events, my father and I grew closer but we were both fiercely protective of our own identities and he bristled if he was referred to as Young Nicoll the piper's father.

My father was the best at what he did and fiercely proud. Through all the years of the war, he and my mother performed miracles, producing toys for local kids at Christmas from recycled rubbish and providing food and clothing when there was little to be had. I can remember a full bridal gown made from a parachute smuggled out of some RAF camp and I wore a winter coat made from an army blanket.

Often my parents would pile rubbish on the kitchen table. Things like buttons, soup cans, pieces of rope, empty cotton reels, odd lumps of wood and scraps of cloth and we would all sit round and try to suggest what could be made from them. My mother could spin thread and weave cloth, make dyes from plants and my father could work wonders with wood. My father believed you could make anything from wood and we supped our porridge and soups from wooden bowls he turned, sat on chairs and dined at a table all of his making. He made intricate wooden jewellery and invented a wooden cigarette lighter and an incredible wooden bottle opener. I was scared to ask for a bicycle when I was at primary school in case he made me a wooden one but when I won a bursary to the Harris Academy at the other end of Dundee I would have welcomed any kind of transport because it was an hour and half walk each way.

The Harris Academy had been a fee paying school prior to the year I started and was situated in an area where each house seemed as big as a whole tenement, with everyone having a room to themselves and bathrooms with inside toilets. I mingled with the children from these homes and marvelled that people had fruit in a bowl when there was nobody ill. I realised poor didn't mean inferior and although I was from a poor family and was acutely aware of the resentment towards a boy who came from the other side, I used it to motivate myself, not to be as good as any of them, but to be better at everything.

I hated Latin, but I hoped to enter veterinary college and a pass in the subject was compulsory, so I studied hard even though a particularly arrogant Latin teacher by the name of Conan attempted to disillusion me. He didn't succeed. I feared every period in that man's class and got poor results in the exams, so I prepared a case, and presented it to the Rector, supporting the theory that bad exam results from a pupil who worked hard indicated flawed teaching. I was sent to another Latin teacher who was very much better and my results improved.

When I was fourteen my father secured a management position with a Glasgow handle manufacturer and we moved to a clapped out house in Govan. I was enrolled at Bellahouston Academy. My father spent a year stripping the house to the stone walls and totally rebuilding the interior. It was a magnificent accomplishment but probably initiated the condition that eventually killed him.

Glasgow was full of exciting potential for a young Nicoll and there was a new attraction at White City Stadium, where I spent every penny I could earn as a messenger boy watching the Glasgow Tigers speedway team.

I suppose I was no different from every other boy who dreamed of being a speedway rider and I idolised the riders but realised that categorised me as an enthusiastic spectator when I really wanted to be a participant.

I made friends with the team mechanic, Dick Stewart, by making myself available as a 'Go-For' and he eventually gave me a job on race nights, helping in the pits, and I travelled at weekends to away matches. Dick made good use of my enthusiasm and willingness and I made good use of his tuition. Soon I was capable of rebuilding an engine and became an asset to the team riders. An asset which I bargained off in exchange for borrowed sessions of bikes'on the track.

Six months after arriving in Glasgow I was racing in second half novice events and I was the envy of the other kids at Bellahouston Academy. Although I didn't realise it then, **my ability at this early age to achieve something that appeared out of reach created a mindset that has always served me well.**

I set out in my adult life to be a vet because my father had always kept livestock and he made me regard that profession as something special. He told me a vet always had respect in the community and money in his pocket. He knew that was true because he had a great respect for vets and put quite a lot of his hard earned cash into their pockets. I desperately wanted my father's approval and I desperately tried to be a vet but, in spite of being conscientious in my studies, two things stood in my way. One of them was that veterinary surgery was my father's dream, not mine, and the other was tuberculosis.

Now in an ill fated marriage, from the age of nineteen I spent fourteen months in Ashludie Sanatorium in Monifeth and only just survived by the final scraps of skin on my six stone frame with the introduction of streptomycin. The doctor's prognosis was a life of incapacity, and my family accepted this, so I discharged myself from hospital and proved I could survive in the real world with a series of poorly paid but interesting jobs such as window cleaning, furniture salesman, farm labouring, morning milk delivery and bin boy. As time went by I convinced the doctors I was fit enough to handle a regular job and worked for a short term as an apprentice saw doctor before returning to study, this time as a zoologist

Traditional jazz was in vogue amongst the student fraternity in the mid-fifties and I successfully operated a band agency when I wasn't studying. This made me financially independent and improved my lifestyle considerably although I would have preferred to play in one of the bands. I did tootle on a trumpet and strum on a banjo but every band I formed asked me to manage them and then replaced me in the line up. I did, on one occasion, make a substantial first night impression on an audience with a new band called the 'Dirty Pigs' but the drummer leapt up to take a bow after a solo and head butted the bell end of my trumpet thereby removing the front teeth so essential to a budding horn player.

My first well paid job was as the 'Pet Man' on Scottish Television's children's programme *Roundabout* and my zoology studies went downhill from there. I became semi-famous as a folk singer in the same era that spawned Billy Connolly, Hamish Imlach, Barbara Dickson etc. and I got married. My best paid job was script writing for comedian Norman Wisdom and the strangest twist occurred when a play I wrote for a London theatre led to a study of behavioural psychology. I ended up touring for years, performing to capacity audiences, techniques that everyone insisted was stage hypnosis but I know was something else.

When business friends asked me to address their employees and explain how I motivated myself I was flattered and realised others perceived me as having some special knowledge or ability that could be valuable to others. What was referred to in the U.S.A. as Personal Reinvention, Personal Development and Self Motivation seemed just natural to me but I decided to study the subject and I went to America and obtained their 'Charter in Motivational Sciences'. I have been to America many times since and I have become friends with many American exponents of the subject

9

which has led me to realise that whilst the American Motivators are the height by which the world measure the rest, their package doesn't work in Europe. We are not Americans and any technique that relies on blind faith and an unshakeable belief that we are living in the land of dreams will always create resistance outside of the States and most certainly in Scotland.

Scots are traditionally stubborn and, whilst I believe it is our indestructibility that gives us our unique set of core strengths, we are predominantly a race of stubborn Scots.

Americans are not, however, just Americans. Oh no. Americans are cowboys or indians, gangsters or movie stars. American accents are internationally recognised through the movie industry as the Southern drawl of Jimmy Stewart or the Bronx bark of Bogey and Cagney whilst symbols such as Chevvies and Harleys are immediate proof of status.

When I visit America I never fail to be impressed with the motivation of the American people. Even the poorest of them believe that theirs is the land of dreams and that achievement is inheritance. The finest seminars, motivation systems and schools of positivity are of American origin and the multitude of books, audio and video personal and corporate development products that circulate the civilised world today are predominantly created by the great American gurus of the 'Be the Best' circus. Nowhere outside the U.S.A. do you find such mass support and practice of PMA. (Positive Mental Attitude) - Why ?

Americans truly believe that everyone else in the world would really like to be American and they feel very special. Most other nationalities who visit America are obliged to endorse these attitudes and so perpetuate the special feeling of being American.

I know I have upheld, vehemently, the patriotic Scottish insistence that, "There's damn few like us and they're aw dee'd!" Realistically, what is it that we are so helluva proud of in our Scottish character?

I have no problem with the scenery. In that department we have it made. I am talking characteristics.

Take sport for instance, Americans have three major spectator sports and they are all very big revenue areas but I have yet to read of an American Football, Basketball or Baseball team buying a player from another country. On the contrary, any player who isn't born in the States and makes it into one of the major league teams is considered very privileged indeed and young boys in America relate to and respond to the recognition that hard work can lead to a career, a reputation and a fortune.

In Scotland our big money football clubs buy from abroad and our baby boys, seeing an ever diminishing platform for their talents, accordingly relate this to national inadequacy and respond to it with diminishing efforts.

I do not accept that we do well in the world arena by being sporting losers or fighting to the end. Sure I accept that there sre certain geographic benefits for a skier to be born or to live in Switzerland but I, like the rest of the world, have watched wee men from deprived backgrounds in Ethiopia running the best in the world into the ground. Where were all the training advantages there? Where was the masses of funding that our sports organisers tell us they need to produce champions. I say these are excuses and everything we need to produce champions in any discipline is in our heart and in our mind. Give me the opportunity and I guarantee Scottish born people can win gold on the sports field, world cups in the team events and accolades in any other field of human endeavour but never ask me to do it for people who don't believe it is possible.

I have now studied personal development in great depth, read many books, attended countless seminars, interviewed hundreds of successful people and listened to multitudes of different theories. I have created my personal style of assisting people by sharing my thoughts and experiences and breaking down my practices and philosophies into working techniques.

The realisation that we can be anything we want to be has been an inspiring and exciting revelation for me. I trust it will be an equally motivational prospect for you!

I've reached an age where I don't just believe in miracles.
I depend on them

(My sentiments entirely)

Watt Nicoll MSP

WHAT DO YOU SEE IN THIS PICTURE

Please do not turn the page but rather answer immediately
without any time to think why you are being asked to answer.

Once you have answered please turn the page

WHAT DO YOU SEE IN THIS PICTURE

Please do not turn the page but rather answer immediately
without any time to think why you are being asked to answer.

Once you have answered please turn the page

WHAT DO YOU SEE IN THIS PICTURE

Please do not turn the page but rather answer immediately
without any time to think why you are being asked to answer.

Once you have answered please turn the page

PICTURE ONE

If you answered 'dogs' – then I would now ask you to return to that picture and identify how many different breeds of dog are in the picture and, once you have identified them and written them down, I would like you to identify their characteristic differences i.e. Greyhounds are fast, Bull terriers are vicious, Poodles are cute etc. etc.

If you have already answered by individually identifying the breeds in their own rights as opposed to grouping them all as dogs, you are off to a flying start in my book. If you have totally identified only one dog then you should ask yourself why and realise that your mindset on dogs has become deficient through programming limitation and some life experience which has identified that breed as more meaningful or interesting. The problem is that you have eliminated all the others from consideration. How many other areas in your life does that apply to?

PICTURE TWO

If you answered 'Trees' – Please return to the picture and identify as many trees as possible and then establish their individual characteristics i.e. Apple trees bear fruit, Oak trees have a very distinctive and strong appearance, Willows bow down and touch the ground etc. etc.

PICTURE THREE

If you answered 'People' would you please return to the picture and establish that there are male people and female people. People of varying heights and assorted dress. This is only the immediate and obvious difference but, once you got to know any one of the people in this picture you would establish their parentage, their environment, their dreams and their experiences and you would realise that they are all totally unique and very much individuals.

Just like the dogs and the trees, at first sight, we are all just people but, looking closer, we are original and unique individuals and it is the recognition of our own uniqueness, our own strengths and weaknesses and our own abilities that will not only allow us to realise our specific area of greatness but to become more tolerant and understanding of all others who are not just people but are original human beings.

Understand this and you understand Universal Law.

CHAPTER ONE

The Person in the Mirror

I HAVE GIVEN YOU a very broad description of who I am and how I arrived at where I am now. I think I have a good idea of my strengths and weaknesses and I will share a few more in depth experiences with you throughout the book. When I look in the mirror I am prepared to accept what I see and I am prepared to recognise that what I see is todays' version. It can be a happy man, a father, a worried man, a husband, a son, a friend, a victim or a hero etc. etc. They are all there in the mirror and I have the ability to call up whichever one I choose to talk to. I am extremely interested in who I am.

Do you know who you are?

Most people choose to live in an imaginary world rather than accept the world as it really is and the result is disillusionment, disappointment and a feeling of always being treated unfairly.

Fairness is an illusion!

Fairness is a fantasy concept people use to excuse themselves from their inadequacies.

Life is never fair!   Life is fact!

We are not all born equal and we are not guaranteed a 'Fair crack of the Whip' but we are all born with the potential to either crack the whip or have it cracked over us! It is just a question of whether you realise your potential and take advantage of your opportunities or chose to whimper when someone else cracks the whip and you are forced to jump.

Always remember that there is no such thing as a wasted opportunity. If you don't take it someone else will and if you don't' use your potential to maximise your life, someone else will, sure as hell, use your life to maximise their potential.

I was born in Scotland, have lived the majority of my life in Scotland and therefore think like a Scot and for better or worse, behave like a Scot.

I am fully aware that different accents exist in Scotland which, to the tuned ear, separate the citizens of Glasgow from the citizens of Edinburgh and I accept that when I travel abroad I am, to all and sundry, a Scot. I am a Scot to an American just as all waiters in Tandoori restaurants are Indian to me.

I was born into the home of a hero, a man amongst men, because my father had fought and bettered Buffalo Bill. So my father told me as an infant and, as Buffalo Bill never made an appearance in Dundee throughout my childhood, I decided it was possibly because he feared my dad. I accepted the fact and gloried in it.

My dad was bald and, when I was a wee boy, my mother used to tell me it was because he never ate his crusts when he was wee. She told me that if I ate all my crusts I would have curly hair when I grew up. I loved my Mum and I accepted what she said as true because it came out of the mouth of the most trustworthy person in my life.

Although I hated crusts and had sufficient intellect to know that, thick or thin, brown or white, crusts had nothing to do with hair, I was still eating crusts when I was twenty eight. I am bald! Probably because my father was bald or because I used a bad shampoo but one thing I do know – it is not because I didn't eat my crusts as a child!

My mother lied! She lied to ensure my nutritional welfare but it is typical of the way we all derive our earliest values and beliefs.

I still burst the bottom of a boiled egg shell when I finish in case a ship sinks at sea and I never cut my nails on Sunday. I do not think I am exceptional in having carried forward deeply ingrained habits and beliefs from my childhood.

My wife punches the pillow every night before going to sleep and only recently admitted she had an inborn fear of going to sleep without punching the pillow because she had seen her mother do it when she was an infant.

By now I hope you are contemplating some of your own seemingly ridiculous practices that either your partner finds amusing or you execute behind locked doors lest your partner finds out.

Take time to contemplate this and write down superstitions, beliefs (possibly self-limiting) and attitudes that you have brought from your childhood and still practise.

Our earliest impressions have an effect on every other piece of information that we absorb throughout life and these early impressions can blind us or even jaundice our opinion. An elder brother, some other kid you hero worshipped, a particularly friendly auntie or a school teacher. Perhaps the wisdom of someone you never even met but studied through the columns of the press. Is it possible you now recognise the influences of your own family and can relate to their teachings. Once you accept this and then question it you open the lid on your own values and your own perceived limitations; the subconscious thoughts and fears, the hopes and dreams you refer to whenever you are faced with either a challenge or an opportunity.

My mother worked to supplement my father's wages and both of them did extra jobs at home because we were poor.

'Poor' was not a word we used however.

My father described himself as a craftsman and my mother described us as respectable. My father took great pride in wearing his good suit (I never remember seeing the bad one) on a Sunday, and my mother took great pride in making sure that when it was her turn to clean the communal stairs, they were cleaned thoroughly.

Oh yes we were a clean family, an honest household, and a credit to ourselves and to our neighbours and I grew up feeling respectable, clean and honest because the people I trusted not only said these words but they lived the part and so did I, until I was old enough and successful enough to look back, re-evaluate it all and recognise the truth.

We were poor!

You may not want to lord it over anyone else, but it doesn't follow that you are incapable of pulling rank or exercising control over another person and it most certainly does not mean that others share your reluctance to wield power.

It is because we don't want to take advantage of anybody that we develop a mind-set that says anybody who does disadvantage another person is unfair and then, when it happens to us, we feel we have been wronged. If we accept that not everyone thinks the same and that it is very possible that someone will take advantage of us, then we wont feel unfairly treated but rather accept the role we have chosen in life.

It bears repeating so I will say it again. If you don't' take control of your own life and use it to your advantage then there is a reasonable chance that someone else will use it to their advantage.

Say Hello to You!

When I am conducting development workshops I always break the participants down into groups based on their natural characteristics then invite them to take stock of where they are, who they are numbered with, and what they think about their own kind.

You can try this exercise on your own or have some fun by trying it in the workplace, with the family or a group of friends.

When I use this technique I am always asked whether it applies to the work situation or the home circumstances. The very fact that the question has to be asked proves that a great many people have different behaviour patterns for the workplace and for the home or social life. The answer to this is straight forward. We usually show more respect for those we know least.

You take the instance of a colleague at work rushing to take a seat ahead of you. In your mind that person may appear arrogant, selfish and ignorant but you smile and indicate that you are happy to find another seat. At home, one of the family beats you to the seat normally recognised as yours and you never hesitate to tell them to move their butt – and quick.

We always hurt the ones we love

For the purpose of the exercise I want you to neither dwell on work or home but rather think of your reactions in general.

To start with you must accept my definition of four words.

EXTROVERT	ANALYTICAL
INTUITIVE	INTROVERT

By EXTROVERT I do not imply you are the ultimate party animal and within fifteen minutes of accessing a party you are to be found on top of the table waving your knickers in the air. For the purpose of this exercise I define EXTROVERT as someone who is outgoing, capable of stating their opinion, extremely confident and comfortable even in a strange environment or with total strangers.

By INTROVERT I am not labelling anyone as a shrinking violet but rather endowing them, with a quiet recognition and acceptance which permits them to have an opinion without having to ram it up everybodys' nose.

First part of this exercise is to make a decision, based on the above definitions, as to whether you are EXTROVERT or INTROVERT

I would describe an ANALYTICAL person as someone who requires loads of detail and information about anything before they would make a decision or take responsibility for it.

An INTUITIVE goes on 'Gut Feeling'. If the vibes are there and it has a good feel to it, if it appeals and excites they would go for it.

Second part of the exercise is to decide, based again on my definitions, whether you are an ANALYTICAL or an INTUITIVE person.

A If you are INTROVERT and ANALYTICAL you will probably recognise that you are perceived by others as :

> DEEP THINKING
> PATIENT
> DELIBERATE

This category do not respond to time restriction but rather relate to perfection. They like plenty information, are natural planners who are committed to excellence.

B If you are EXTROVERT and ANALYTICAL you will probably recognise that you are perceived by others as :

> ASSERTIVE
> DRIVEN
> CONTROLLING

This category seldom see the need to discuss or negotiate with others and are generally poor listeners because they think it is rediculous to waste time discussing something when they know the answer. They are very focussed and totally time driven, bottom line people who do not suffer fools.

They normally get their way in everything – **or declare war!**

C If you are INTROVERT and INTUITIVE you will probably recognise that you are perceived by others as :

> CONSIDERATE
> LOVING AND CARING
> TRUSTWORTHY

This category care more for people than material goods. These are nature lovers and extremely capable of making the best of a bad lot. They tend to have everything put onto them and are regularly taken advantage of, but they find it easy to forgive their tormentors.

Natural team players who always respond to a caring and considerate approach.

D If you are EXTROVERT and INTUITIVE you will probably recognise that you are perceived by others as :

> HIGHLY MOTIVATED
> CHEERFUL
> GOOD FUN
> HELPFUL

This category respond well to a convivial atmosphere and see life as for living to the full. They take it upon themselves to spread sunshine wherever they go and are excellent team workers, very supportive of others and always enthusiastic.

Very seldom do we acknowledge the fact that we display identifiable characteristics and recognising them can serve to either boost our moral or depress us. Imagine finding yourself identified with a group of people who are behaving in a manner you find totally unacceptable and then realising that, as you see them, others see you.

You will tend to revert to your natural characteristics when you are either very relaxed or under intense pressure as opposed to the characteristics you will demonstrate in your preferred state.

You may be, by nature, quiet and withdrawn and very comfortable keeping yourself and your opinions to yourself, but your job requires an outgoing flamboyance and promotion depends on your ability to sell yourself. Your preferred characteristics would be that of a sunny, cheerful, chatty chappie. Great! You only have to observe such a personality, model yourself on them, get over the embarrassment and, in a very short space of time, you will be able to mimic and enjoy all the benefits of the natural extrovert.

One small incident irritates the boss and he calls you out very publicly branding you a loudmouth and a big-head.

Zapp! – You revert to your natural self and spring back into the comfort zone of your natural characteristics.

Make a List of Your Natural Characteristics.

Make a list of Your Preferred Characteristics.

Start to Recognise the Difference.

> *We are all born equal but we are not born the same.*

Want to try another Evaluation?

Do you understand the intended purpose of what you have read so far?

- Was the purpose achieved?
- Was the message relevant to you?
- Can you use this information?
- Will you use this information?
- How will you use this information?
- Where and when will you use it?

Dependent on how far down that list you answered positively you should now choose from:

- Progress to the next stage
- Read the previous chapter again
- Pass the book on to someone you don't like

Chapter Two

Do You Know What You Want?

A REGULAR WORKSHOP starting point for me would be to ask every attendee to establish what it is they want from the session. I establish this, then ask everyone what they want that week, then what they want that year and ultimately what they want out of life. Then I give them the Mission Statement!

"You can have anything you want, be anything you want to be, do anything you want to do if you can satisfy three very simple conditions".

> *You have to know what you want.*
> *You have to know why you want it.*
> *You have to believe it is achievable.*

Very few know what they want. What they really, really want. Most of us never really give *quality time* to the consideration.

In my search for that special something that sets the successful minority apart from the majority, I have interviewed hundreds of people who are perceived to be successful. I was fascinated with a series of facts that didn't equate. I couldn't relate top of the range cars and designer clothing with someone who was self made yet apparently uneducated, and often downright thick. I found it difficult to determine what exactly it was that took people with minimal advantage on to the highest rung whilst smart, good look-ing, highly intelligent and family connected aspirants ended up holding the ladder.

I decided to study the successful, to research their background and history, and, where possible, talk to them. I convinced myself there would be a common denominator somewhere in their make-up and I would locate this, develop it, market it, and join them at the top.

The first discovery I made was basic. Success is not necessarily measurable in terms of wealth. Success is personal to the individual and can be anything from large quantities of cash to contentment. I first had to determine exactly what success is and define it in a way that could be instantly acceptable to everyone. Here are some of the ingredients I claim are essential and are part of every successful person I have ever met or researched.

A Clear Conscience – No matter how powerful, wealthy, intelligent or good looking you are. If you do not have a clear conscience, in my book, you are not successful. I met and have heard of so many who did so much to get what they wanted only to find their conscience gave them no peace to enjoy the fruits of their efforts.

Health – Right behind a clear conscience, I value health and the physical ability to participate in life to the full. Not everyone can enjoy perfect health and some are less fortunate than others in their inherited abilities, but I think successful people maximise and recognise the benefits of maintaining a level of health and fitness with disciplined diet and exercise.

Quality Relationships is an essential success quotient. How you relate to other people and how other people relate to you. Just think of the stress that comes from bad relationships at work, within the family, anywhere. It is a well established fact that most of our real troubles speak back to us. In other words they come from other people. They come from a breakdown in communication or conflicting views within a relationship. Successful people relate well to other people and, if you are now challenging the credibility of my research by nominating some incredibly wealthy tycoon who would easily qualify as Bastard of the Year, let me respond by questioning the correlation of wealth to success.

If you have a clear conscience, good health, quality relationships and still cannot classify yourself as one of the successes of life, let me now enter the area most commonly associated with success by those who don't have it.

Money! The stuff that buys the goodies that impresses the many who envy the few.

Money is an undeniable necessity for success. I am regularly confronted by those who insist they are not interested in cash and I personally have other motivational buttons, but, we all live in a society where the recognised evaluation in the exchange and acquisitions of things essential to survival are measured by money.

'Love flies out the window when poverty comes through the door.' Heard it? Believe it! Healthy diets cost money and basic needs create bills which have to be paid. Wealth, however, is not essential to success. On the contrary, I have encountered those who are wealthy and friendless because they mistrust the intentions of everyone and their fortune only brings stress into their lives.

Stress free, peace of mind can be maintained with financial stability and that I interpret as being in possession of sufficient money to eliminate the worry about money. This amount will, of course, vary with every individual and, whilst Richard Branson might require a few bob more to keep his balloon up in the air, Jimmy Bloggs could be a very successful suburban on the kind of loose change Mr. Branson throws out of his balloon in coppers for the waving throngs.

Successful people have a clear conscience, they maximise their health, have good relationships and enough money passing through their hands to maintain their' preferred lifestyle. I could give you a whole number of other ingredients such as self esteem because, if you don't like yourself you haven't really been very successful, however I will contain my finding to that which can be most immediately and effectively purposeful to those who seek success.Every successful person knows what they want. They are not vague about this with wimpish broad generalisations such as 'I just want to be happy'. We all want to be happy. Let's all be happy and have a happy, happy world. The difference is that the successful person knows exactly what it would take to make them happy and, if they don't, they would make it their business to find out.

If you don't know where you are going how can you tell when you get there? The next item, and possibly the most important piece of equipment in the success toolbox, is to have desired outcomes.

You have to know what you want. You have to know where you want to go. You have to know why you want what you want and why you want to go where you want to go. You have to want it with a passion and you have to fuel that passion by visualising yourself as an achiever, as having reached your own personal goals with good health, a clear conscience, good relationships and no financial concerns plus whatever the more personal factors of your desired outcomes include.

Naturally, everyone would like to live at the top of the hill and share the good things that are bubbling over at the top of the two horns of plenty whilst the majority have to exist on a share of the pathetic wee drop at the bottom of the cone.

Ask anyone who lives at the top of the hill how you get there and you will find they are confused by the question. The work, the discipline and the effort to reach that stage just came natural to them but, if you really want to know how to get to the top, ask anyone who lives at the bottom of the hill and they will tell you. They all

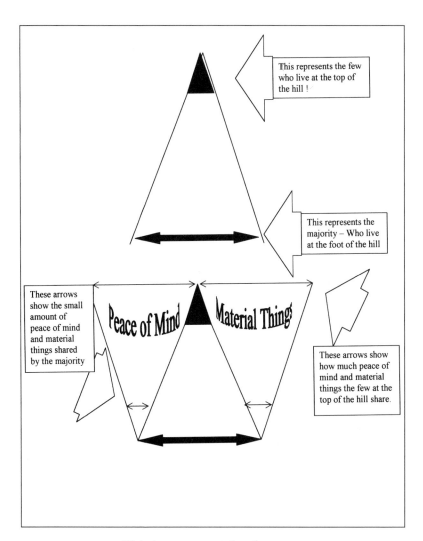

Labels within the figure:

- This represents the few who live at the top of the hill!
- This represents the majority – Who live at the foot of the hill
- These arrows show the small amount of peace of mind and material things shared by the majority
- These arrows show how much peace of mind and material things the few at the top of the hill share.

Peace of Mind / Material Things

This is my mountain of success

know. They live at the bottom of the hill, they envy those who live at the top of the hill but they don't do anything about it even though they know how the others reached that desirable height.

Easy – The folks at the bottom of the hill know the others reached the top because they were lucky!

Luck is when opportunity surpasses preparation.

If you want a thing bad enough
To go out and fight for it
To work day and night for it
To give up your time – your peace
  And your sleep for it

If all that you dream – and scheme
  Is about it
If life seems useless and worthless
  Without it
And if you'd rather sweat for it
And plan for it and fret for it
And lose all your terror of the opposition for it
And if you simply go after that thing that you want
With all your capacity
Strength and sagacity
Faith, hope and confidence
  And stern perspicacity

If neither poverty nor hardship
Can banish your goal
Sickness or pain – of body or brain
Can keep you away from the
Thing that you want
When all was looking grim
You kept sight of your chin
When your belief says you can
Though all others say you – *can't*
When you deserve what you get
  You'll get what you want!

This is something I got from Les Brown. He is a good motivator.
If he was Scottish he would be perfect.

Desired Outcomes

I bought my computer from a High Street store complete with software, which was originated in America. It spells in American and selects synonyms from an American thesaurus and, like the majority of personal development products originated and developed in the States, it is probably powerful medicine in its' own environment but requires understanding, patience and a total translation before it even begins to cut the mustard in 'Oor Toon'. One good thing the American encyclopaedia produced for me, however, was a great word I had never heard before **Teleology**.

Teleology is apparently the **'Study of Purpose'** or, in every day language of the Non American – the benefit of having desired outcomes.

The belief that living organisms can only be properly understood in terms of their purposes.

The supportive material was based on the quality and success of our life depending on whether the goals we have are chosen by us, or whether we have allowed others, or circumstances, to choose our goals for us.

I believe this aspect of our nature is extremely important and, without desired outcomes, we survive under the influence of other people or events and at best fade away and die in ignorance of what our potential or purpose was. We may sense there should be more to life than two beetroots on your chips when it's your birthday and start believing that there really are cowboys and it is possible to become a cowboy before we self destruct.

Anybody who has ever seen a James Bond movie knows that guided missiles are target seeking by magnetism, sound, heat etc. Unlike a bullet, they can alter course as their target shifts. They have a scanning device which corrects them when they are off course and my son impressed me when he was eleven-years-old by explaining that it works on negative feed back.

We are all very impressed with this modern technology and yet very few realise that our own brain is much more sophisticated than any electro magnetic device and we have the ability to redirect, recharge, resurge and home in on our programmed target with much more dedicated and deadly accuracy than any military device.

Because we have the subliminal awareness of this personal potential, we become anxious and upset, not only when we fall below what we have visualised as our standards of performance or what we consider 'good enough', but we also get upset when we do better than we expected.

This strange phenomena that upsets us when we feel we are doing better than we are entitled to in life is the reason why so many lottery winners just literally throw the money away and why people appear to deliberately sabotage their promotion . They just cannot accept that they are entitled to be living that quality of life and the discomfort drives them to lifestyle destruction.

Human propulsion is generated when the brain compares **Present Reality** with a Visualisation or **Desired Outcome**. Or The Goal we have set. It is the gap between what we have/where we are and what we want to have and where we want to be that motivates us and generates the energy.

Try writing down what you have in the left hand column of a sheet of paper and then, in the right hand column, write what you would like to have. Do the same with the other categories I have listed, then spend a few minutes comparing the left hand column with the right hand column and register the effect of this exercise on your thinking process, your attitude and your general disposition.

What you have	compared to	What you want to have
What you can do	compared to	What you want to do
What you are	compared to	What you want to be
Where you are	compared to	Where you want to be

What you have just experienced is a self induced acceleration of the normal wish fulfilment process which is the instigator of motivation and the fuel that maintains the forward thrust towards the goal.

It is essential to have clarity and detail in your desired outcomes because, if present reality is brighter and more instantly appealing than your dream, then you will fall back on present reality.

We always move towards the dominant picture.

Desired Outcome Analyses

Now try answering the following questions. Some of them may be a little painful and you may even wonder why some of them are even relevant but, as you are under no obligation to share the information with another living soul, why not give it your best possible shot.

What is your uppermost goal in life?

The one thing you are determined to achieve

Where do you spend most of your time?

With whom do you spend most of your time?

Think well and be truthful – The answer may well surprise even you.

What do you talk about most?

Are your words and actions consistent with your major goal?

Is the person you spend most time with an important part of your quest or are they even aware of your personal ambition?

What is your family/social group's major purpose?

This one can hurt but consider well what your innermost thoughts are and recognise the truth. Are they an essential support or are they a liability, a feel good factor or an embarrassment?

What is the big current challenge in your life?

What attitudes, habits, beliefs, comfort zones, self talk and goals need to be adjusted to overcome this challenge?

What are your three top goals, currently?

What attitudes, habits, beliefs, comfort zones, self talk need to be adjusted to achieve these goals?

Goal Setting (The Rules)

Your goals must be aligned to your own personal values and beliefs. Having a goal to start your own business whilst placing security as your number one value could create conflict.

Goals must be written down to commence the process of turning the invisible into the visible.

It's just a thought until you put it into action and the first and easiest action is to write it down.

Understand why you want to attain a particular goal. Writing down the reasons will help you to evaluate them and get the experience of achieving them.

If you cannot add detail to your vision of the desired outcome there is no *because* and the goal is unlikely to inspire you:

Review your goals regularly. Most people set goals at the start of a year and review them at the end of the year.

Reviewing your goals monthly increases your chances of achieving them times twelve.

Reviewing your goals weekly enhances their power times fifty two.

Reviewing your goals once a day means there is three hundred and sixty five times more resolve behind them.

Your goals must be inspirational to you and attainable by you and should not be dependent on others.

Be specific. How does your goal look, feel, sound, smell and taste? The more of your senses you apply, the more your brain will support your desire to succeed.

It is important to avoid conflicting circumstances in your life. The following areas should be considered when setting any goal:

social, family. spiritual. financial, career

plus any other category applying to you personally.

Suppose a man is prepared to work day and night at some boring task in order to accumulate enough capital to permit him to retire aged forty, buy a small beach bar in the Mediteranean and live out his life in sun drenched semi-retirement. This is his goal. This is his dream. This is what he rises each day and works hard to achieve. This is quality goal setting and highly motivational – for him!

Let us now consider his good lady wife, whom he sincerely wishes to spend his life and grow old with. This woman has her desired outcomes too. She dreams of buying an idyllic country cottage in Caithness to be closer to her mother.

Both have good motivating goals but they are conflicting and more likely to fragment the quality of life than enhance it.

Start your goal-setting process assuming you cannot fail. Excite yourself by allowing your imagination to run wild then refine the goal at a later point.

Never set negative goals. Rather state what you intend to achieve than something you intend to avoid.

Once you have decided on your goals and ensured they do not conflict with any other area of your life, heap on detail upon detail until you are virtually experiencing the desired outcome.

Actual Goal Setting

It starts with a thought!

Everything in life starts with a thought. Every single day in life we have thousands of thoughts but that is all they are – Just a thought. Occasionally we do something about what we think about and the bridge between thought and action is what we call motivation.

- Identify exactly what you want.
- Write it down.
- Identify why you want it.
- Write it down.
- Write down why you want to reach each goal.
- List the obstacles, difficulties and challenges you foresee.
- List the people, organisations and groups you will require to work with.
- Identify what information you require and what you need to learn.
- Develop a plan of action.
- Set a date of achievement.
- Break a Long Term Goal down into believable/achievable increments.

Once you have established these facts and truly understand why you want something, you recognise that it is achievable and your self limiting beliefs start to fall away.

You never again have to answer the mental hell hound with the repetitious, nagging question "Can I do it"?

You will know you can do it and the only question that requires an answer is :

Do I want to do it?

Goal Setting

Creating lists of skills you require, supportive organisations, essential contacts, necessary actions, beneficial reading material etc.

Goal setting should intensify focus but, invariably, counter strategies from other areas of life dilute the strength of resolve and it is therefore essential to spend quality time on realistic goal setting to embrace the strategies and commitments within other areas of life.

Strategies:

- How to change circumstances.
- Pitfalls (Courting failure).

- Negotiating for what you want.
- Being assertive without being unpleasant.
- Power of Persuasion.
- Establishing a system of regular feedback and assessment.
- Understanding and Controlling Attitude.
- Home Life.
- Intimate Relationships.

You have to visualise these goals adding more and more details until the reality of your dreams become something you are totally familiar with, something you know exists, is possible and believable.

Then, and only then, you will have the same mindset as success-ful people.

Your desire to touch and hold what has become so special and precious to you, will drive you, motivate and energise you, to do all that is necessary to reach that special category.

It is sensationally simplistic but the power of simplicity is awe-some.

You just have to want to be successful enough to do something about it.

You have to set goals within goals.

Immediate goals might be as basic as making enquiries and gleaning information.

Short term goals see you taking the first action.

Mid term goals encourage you to intensify your efforts.

Intermediate goals prevent disillusionment and provide stimu-lus for the final push to whatever you have set your heart on.

Quality goal setting takes time because you have to dig deep within yourself and question your desires.

You have to make certain that what you have set out for yourself really appeals and isn't some mental panacea or a scenario that impresses your partner or your parents or your employer – not even your lover.

It has to be what the real, deep down *you* want out of life.

It has to be something you become passionate about.

Once you have **quality goals**, decisions become easy to make because you know where you are going and you know how to get there.

Decisions are focussed on this outcome.

- Will it take me closer to my goal. Yes or No ?
- Nothing else matters.
- Your goals are the essence of your existence.
- Your reason for being.
- Your major definite purpose in life.
- Yes it will take me closer to my goal.
- **Yes I will do it!**

Once was a man who whistled a tune
As he set out to do what couldn't be done

And he did it!

Why not try another Evaluation?

Do you understand the intended purpose of what you have read so far?
- Was the purpose achieved?
- Was the message relevant to you?
- Can you use this information?
- Will you use this information?
- How will you use this information?
- Where and when will you use it?

Dependent on how far down that list you answered positively you should now choose from:
- Progress to the next stage
- Read the previous chapters again
- Find somewhere quiet to think about what you have just read

CHAPTER THREE

Good is a Bad Word

GOOD IS A POOR GOAL and *best* is an unrealistic goal because it defies improvement. The word for motivated movers is *better*. .

> To be better than you are today
> To do better than you have ever done before
> To be better than the best.

One ingredient which is part of the make up of every successful person I have encountered, whether they are in the corporate world, sports, finance, education or the personal profiles of having reached their 'happy' plateau.

> None of the successful settle for good.
> Good is just that – it is good.
> Good just means *not bad*
> Good is the enemy of *great*

If you aim for peace of mind, the best health available to you, quality relationships, financial freedom, self esteem and realistic goals, you will progress towards all of these things and, somewhere around the mid term goals, you will feel good.

That is good but it is not great and those few you envy didn't settle for the good life. Their goal was to have a better life. The best possible life available.

In Days of Old when Knights were Bold

'Once upon a time', when I was a boy, 'In Days of Old' used to be the traditional starting point for a school playground narration. It was very popular whenever any adult (usually a teacher) did anything to incur the disdain of the young set, a rhyme was penned. The chant always ended by accusing the older person of being contented with second best.

In days of old when the knights were bold
And laws weren't invented
You did as tell't or got the belt
And had to be contented

This kind of composition was a favourite pass-time of mine and I think children are particularly receptive to this format of story-telling because it gives license to a feeling of superiority when they are encouraged to visualise a world before the invention or discovery of all the modern technology they now take for granted.

Youngsters just love to be presented with evidence to support many of their views that the adults are a bunch of 'diddies' and to read about a time when they used paraffin lamps to provide light or took six weeks to travel from Edinburgh to London on horseback. That can be a real hoot to kids who flood the home with light at the flick of a switch or have made the fifty minute flight between the two capitals.

Some of the boys' verses got to be quite rude and were usually all the better received because of it because we were living in an enlightened age and could only assume these figures from our past were indeed some kind of 'plonkers' if they didn't recognise how obvious it was that they could have improved their living standard by simply switching on the light.

In days of old when knights were bold
And chewing gum wasn't invented
We picked our nose and chewed on those
And had to be contented.

In days of old when knights were bold
And Delsey wasn't invented
They wiped their arse on a clump of grass
And had to be contented

We were going for laughs, but there is indeed a lesson in Personal Development to be learned from that simple children's poem and a modern version might be:

In days of old when knights were bold
And computers weren't invented
They made up games to exercise their brains
And had to be contented.

Through excercising their brains, some of those knights must surely have got to thinking about alternative forms of energy and eventually invented the means of turning night into day. But it seems to me we don't have to go quite that far back into history to establish the effect of change. I personally don't recall any knights, bold or otherwise, but I can recall a time when life values were considerably different:

> In days of old, so we've been told
> When progress wasn't invented
> The kids left school and worked as a rule
> And most were quite contented.

Now we have a new breed who use discontentment as fuel for ambition. They are people who do not accept personal limitation. They believe the world and all within is there for the taking if you open your mind. They are called *entrepreneurs.*

Definition of the Word *Entrepreneur*

Origin: French.

Noun: Contractor.

Verb: To begin, to launch, to embark upon, to begin a voyage.

Understanding the Application of the Word

An entrepreneur is a person who recognises opportunity, analyses situations, negotiates preferential terms, calculates and minimises risks, sets targets, plans actions and persists in their pursuance. The entrepreneur is internally powered and never externally controlled. Success or failure depends on how he/she handles what life throws at them.

The entrepreneur doesn't deny the reality of situations, doesn't paint rosy pictures but rather dwells on the fact that, where there is a more desirable set of facts than those immediately apparent, there is an opportunity. In short, the entrepreneur doesn't make excuses nor amplify problems but rather seeks the alternative he/she knows must exist.

To be entrepreneurial is to favour internal control and view every effective external factor in your life which can, in any degree, shade your decision as a loss of control.

Every member of society has to accept that government legislation immediately affecting them is an external control, the weather is an external control we all have to concede to. Very often health is a factor over which we have no control, but have you considered that falling in love is to concede your own selfish and personal opinion in favour of a new joint policy and therefore is another external control.

Children are external controls as are any relatives or loved ones we choose to accept responsibility for, and that is the line over which a true entrepreneur will step and the key word here is 'choose'.

How may control factors have you chosen to concede? When that big opportunity came along did you pass it up because you personally wanted to, or did you pass it up because you couldn't be with your partner or didn't know how to break the news to another person?

In days of old when wealth was gold
And equality wasn't invented
The poor had to hike or ride a bike
And never knew they were discontented.

Nobody ever changes anything willingly if they are comfortable with what they have and what they experience.

This was all about control and the majority of working class people had very limited control if indeed any control over day to day living or indeed their own destiny. Income was controlled by pay rates within the local industry and related trade or professional opportunities for personal advancement.

Childhood was controlled by a legislation that dictated which school they attended, how many hours in how many years they attended and the subjects they studied were controlled by national standards set by people on a high plain in a far away place.

Home life was controlled by financial restriction, their sexual life was controlled not only be limited resources for image design (polishing the toe caps of their working boots was as far as some ever got) by geographic and community awareness and their ability to break free from the restrictions was controlled by the dependency of children or ageing parents.

Those early few who broke the mould and became their own boss, took responsibility for their own life, created a personal independence and demonstrated, by example, an alternative way of life were the forerunners to what we now call 'Entrepreneurs'.

Entrepreneurs are people who maintain internal control of their own life. The entrepreneurs' motto could be:

If it's to be, it's up to me

The entrepreneur doesn't expect to be paid just for turning up or putting in hours but they are motivated by the thought of reward for effort! They don't do things because they have to, but rather they choose to, want to, love to – Do it!

Consider your own entrepreneurial attitudes and recognise the superior feel good factor in activities such as passing your driving test. You don't have to be rewarded for learning to drive or play a musical instrument. The achievement is the reward!

Entrepreneurial people are:

Self starters

Accountable

Not buck passers

Looking for solutions not excuses

Full of tremendous energy and drive

Movers and shakers
(forward from current reality to the desired outcome)

How do you score on that list? Write down a score out of twenty for each category and then total them up. If you score less than 100 review your low scoring categories and ask yourself questions:

Am I a poor self starter because I am not excited with my present lifestyle?

Do I avoid accountability because I feel inadequate in my employment?

Do I pass the buck because I resent another or because of pride?

Could I possibly try harder to find solutions?

Did I have more energy when I was doing something that interested me?

Am I really moving towards anything definite or just surviving another day?

Progress was a big word when I was a kid. My father spoke of pro-gress in terms of a five day working week as opposed to the previous six day week. A forty hour working week as further progress, time and a half for work undertaken in excess of his forty hour week as great progress and double time for Sunday work as incredible progress.

My mother, who was a dressmaker, observed progress through the introduction of 'man made' fibres and my aunt considered Preparation H as the ultimate progress in haemoroidal tolerance.

Progress was something to be marvelled at for a while as our lives were changed with the introduction of plastics, biro pens, pressure cookers etc. and then progress became something everyone expected. When doctors failed to issue a magical prescription, if worn road surfaces were not replaced with some new substance or tea breaks were not augmented with tea biscuits then it would be perceived as making 'No Progress' and no progress made people discontented.

When people become discontented they are going through a powerful area of opportunity because they are admitting that they are not satisfied with something and that means that they are aware that it could be improved. Even though they are not yet aware of how it can be improved, they continually dwell on the subject and, when someone becomes obsessed with a subject, they intensify the possibility of thinking up the way or the means to improve it:

> In days of old somebody sold
> Something they had invented
> They opened our eyes to a financial prize
> And made it hard to be contented

The great inventions are well documented and we Scots fair well in this league with Logie Baird, MacAdam, Bell, Watt, Stevenson, Fleming, Chalmers etc. etc. etc.

This is clear evidence of the ability of a human being to use their discomfort and discontent as their spur and starter button for original and innovative thinking.

It is when you feel that insufficient progress is being made in some area of your life, when you feel that unrelenting discontent, that feeling that there must be more to life than just this! That is the magic moment when you are likely to make a discovery. A moment in time when your brain is flooded with realisation and you change your direction, change your attitude, change your habits and you do something to effectively improve the area within which you are experiencing discomfort.

Ask yourself if you are living in a perfect environment. Is there absolutely nothing could be done to improve life in your city, village, town , street or home? If there is anything you feel would make an improvement then there is a business opportunity for an inventor, a service provider or a sales outlet.

Make a list of everything you feel could enhance your environment. Ask your friends to make a list and then marvel at how many business opportunities there are by supplying what others would perceive as progress!

In 1892 the American Patents office was closed and the following announcement publicised

'Everything, worth inventing has been invented'

March , 1949

Where the latest calculator on the ENIAC system is equipped with 18,000 vacuum tubes and weighs thirty tons, computers of the future may eventually have only 1,0000 vacuum tubes and could, some day, weigh as little as one and a half tons.

(Editor) – *Popular Mechanics*

THE BIRTH OF THE LAPTOP

The IT Age

This is the era of IT (Information Technology). The future depends on electronic mail, computer literacy and the microchip. The world is currently being united by this age of Intelligent Technology but I think we have had the IT family for centuries and most certainly as long as I lived.

We had the Its in the street where I was born, I went to school with them, through higher education, travelled all over the country with them and meet them to this day most places I go.

There was a whole family of Its' and they appear to be prolific breeders but I most vividly recall the triplets SEEN IT, DUNN IT and HEARD IT.

No matter how I tried to do something new or original it appeared the Its' could top me and disillusion me at every turn. If I described somewhere my father had taken me at the weekend – SEEN IT – totally defused the excitement.

The most outrageous joke was rendered as funny as two carobuncles in the back passage by – HEARD IT. Whilst my wildest possible projected intentions paled into insignificance in the presence of – DUNN IT.

These are the NEGGIE ITS' but there is another family of ITS' who are the positives and are obviously in no way related to the negative ITS'.

The POSSIES, who invariably sport the same first names, are supportive and enthusiastic about their fellow creatures and tend to appear when you have self doubts. I.e. You are telling a crowd of doubters about a holiday offer you heard on the radio for which you have sent the cheque off. It seems like an unbelievable opportunity for a visit to paradise for the price of a local bus fare. The listeners ridicule the possibility of such an offer being genuine, question your sanity for parting with the cash and, when you endeavour to shade it all with credibility by quoting the radio as your source, they even imply you are lying. Suddenly they are silenced by HEARD IT, who invariably is supported by SEEN IT and DUNN IT all applauding your actions and recounting, in a positive and supportive manner, their experience with the same company the previous year.

Be careful when you are euphorically uplifted by the POSSIES because they have a French connection with a stilted vocabulary. They are the BEENAIRS.

The BEENAIRS are sometimes Possies but much more often they are practising MONO-NEGGES – One Expression, One Point of View, One Body Movement, One Word Vocabulary. They shake their head as though in constant disbelief that it is still there, and deliver their total contribution to the conversation –'Beenair'.

To be a POSSIE is often a great frustration because positive attitude, support and information is often perceived as insincere, condescending and even insulting. I truly believe we all protect ourselves from the hurt of disappointment by resisting positive people (The Black Abbot), by refusing to be led to a higher place from which we might tumble.

It is my own opinion that this resistance to positive attitude is a direct result of the social practice of acceptable lying. Many of our children are almost encouraged to accept this practice with advice like, 'When Auntie Flossie asks if you would like another cake – you say no.'

The wee person receiving that kind of life instruction will eventually grow up incapable of ever making an honest response which would first deal with the accurate pertinence of the question, then support the immediate response with credible reason, before delivering a definitive conclusion.

'You kidding? I would like the whole plate cause they're brilliant so they are, no hard baps like yours Maw.'

The reason we find good news hard to believe is because we are a society of liars. How about: 'The cheque's in the post.' 'I was just about to phone you' then think about the most prolific lies in your immediate world. Social small talk is invariably blatant lying.

'Morning Fred. How are you today'?

'First Class Joe. Yourself'?

'Great Fred.'

A conversation like that takes place in our society millions of times every day. Quite often the Fred character throws himself out a twenty story window two hours later and Joe recounts how cheery he appeared when they exchanged their morning health check. The truth is, both of them felt dreadful but both realised that the other didn't really give a toss how the other felt and, had either one of them taken the time to tell the truth about how they felt, they would have been branded a BB (Boring Being would you believe – No ? – Well I did say we are all liars).

I recently visited a Primary School in Lanarkshire where the chapel bell was ringing its head off at eight in the morning as I drove through the gates and joined the earlier members of the staff running towards the bell tower. We found a ten-year-old boy virtually being lifted off his feet as he clung to the louping bell rope. Still being lifted up and down and obviously caught in the act, his immediate response was, 'It wasnae me.'

We readily accept that women lie about their age, even joke about it, and why not. A womans' age is a very acceptable lie and most men are more than happy to play within the rules of this game. A thirty five year old natural blonde size eight is, in reality, probably a forty year old, mousey brown, size twelve shovelled into a carefully selected garment that perpetuates the preferred image.

All of that is perfectly acceptable social lying girls because we men also tell lies and we all know they are lies but accept them from others because we use them ourselves. It may shock you to learn that men tell lies about the size of their willies.

I totally agree with this area of social untruths because I want to believe I am chatting to a thirty-five-year-old size eight and will always enhance the exchange by swearing I had taken her for a thirty-year-old who must surely have her wardrobe made to measure with such a beautiful figure.

I know that they know I am lying and they know that I know they are lying but we both feel the better for it. I call this kind of exchange

VERBAL COSMETICS and I truly feel that some exchange of complimentary observation will do a great deal more for the average make or female than any cosmetic which is physically applied. I definitely do not want the kind of social change that guarantees everything a person says is gospel, because then I would have to believe the guys who scratch their knee when they talk about their willie.

The truth about the truth is that it is really about much more than the words that are spoken and should be assessed on the body language, attitude and purpose of the person endeavouring to communicate and the preferred message for the listener.

The Scottish Connection

When the Scots went in search of new horizons, they were not afraid to lose sight of their native shoreline for they carried with them an attitude that was indestructable !

The Most Interesting Person in the World

The family sit round the TV watching the news report of a major Gala event. The Presidents of ten major world powers are present and it is attended by the greatest single gathering of world-wide superstars ever to congregate on one occasion.

There is a thousand piece orchestra playing and the highlight is to be the first public appearance of God. The TV cameras scan the crowd and suddenly Mum leaps to her feet in a state of uncontrollable excitement:

'There's Jessie McFarlane. She and I were in the same maternity ward when our Peter was born'.

She is on the phone in an instant to her sister.

'Are you watching the tele? Did you see Jessie McFarlane? She was standing next to the wee man with the brown hair. Remember we were in the maternity at the same time. I don't think that can be her man because she told me he was bald and I know the baby was pure bald when it was born'.

The most interesting thing in the world to any one person is that which they can directly relate to.

It is an essential step on the journey to self fulfilment to recognise and believe that you are the most interesting person in the world and I base this statement on the philosophy that a person can only perform to their maximum potential if they believe in themselves.

The starting point in your PDP (Personal Development Plan) must be self recognition and that comes from being sufficiently interested in yourself, to be aware of:

> Who you are
>
> What you are
>
> Why you are what you are.

As a young folk singer I was one of a group of Scots invited to perform at a Folk Festival in Osnabruck. The year was 1967 and there was still a powerful presence of British army personnel in Germany, which was just as well because we would have been sadly short of an audience had we been dependent on local support for bagpipes, heedrum hodrum and songs with lyrics like:

> 'The bombing raids, the bombing raids
> Made on the boys who made the marmalade.
> Had Hitler only known – The trench was Dundee's own
> He'd have never made the bombing raids'

We undertook the Bremen train journey well prepared with the Scottish folk-singers' support group – Malt Whisky, McEwans Lager and sausages (you just cannot get pies in Germany). The train we travelled in was instantly recognisable as similar to the ones we had seen in so many war movies and the conversation revolved round the 'What if' supposition of over imaginative folkies.

The daylight dwindled in parallel to the contents of our bottles and sleep replaced the conversation, but not the subject matter, as dreams explored a scenario of this same journey through a Germany that had won the war and where jack-booted Gestapo officers with long memories of anti-Nazi songs held the powers of life and death.

I awoke with a start, a demanding bladder, and an uneasy feeling, to find the train had stopped in some remote part of the countryside. I reached for the whisky bottle only to find I had somehow drunk the lot. The night was jet black and I was feeling sick and had a headache. I peered through the window and considered the possible option that I hadn't wakened and this was the worst part of the dream. There were soldiers in the field surrounding the train.

I have no problem with soldiers. Soldiers very often demonstrate a high degree of focus and self discipline and are, to my mind, much less threatening than an indeterminate gang of yobos' at a street corner, who have no identifiable purpose in life, but these were German soldiers, instantly recognisable by their steel helmets and the sub machine gun slung over the shoulder.

Anyone who can remember the old black and white war movies would understand what went through my mind as these soldiers entered the train and proceeded to move from seat to seat checking passports.

I relived every scene from the Belsen news reels and temporarily forgot where I had secreted my papers. Closer and closer they came until I found myself staring down the muzzle of a gun. An unsmiling soldier snatched my passport and delivered three questions I have since learned require the three answers which provide the basis, the heart and the engine of every personal development plan.

If I had only realised all these years ago, that serious contemplation of these three questions would have provided me with the kind of understanding that gives life meaning, I truly believe I could have achieved greatness at an early age. Every time I travel abroad and I go through passport control, I remember and use the experience to reappraise my personal standards.

As I squinted into the barrel of that gun, fought to keep my bladder under control, silently vowed never to sing the 'Bombing Raids' in Germany again and prayed I wouldn't be sick, that soldier demanded:

Where do you come from?

Why are you here?

Where are you going?

If you have satisfactory answers to these three questions then your self understanding is absolute and your goals are clear. These are the essential ingredients in personal development. Try now to take the Passport Test.

Where do you come from? This demands you take a close look into your life journey so far, with an honest appraisal of the control factors and circumstances which affected your decisions. Think about it, analyse it and write down why you think you are where you are and are doing what you are doing with your life. Was it a plan or have you just reacted to whatever life threw at you?

Why are you here'? Back to question one – 'Why are you reading this book'? If you are looking into personal improvement or development then it surely must be because you feel things could be better. What things could be better? Why are you discontent? If you are not already an achiever – why are you not discontent?

Where are you going'? If you know what you want and you know why you want it. If you can convince yourself that what you want is achievable then, and only then will you definitely know where you are going!

My idea is to reintroduce each individual to themselves in a positive light and kindle the recognition that they are not only interesting but, within themselves, they will find the most interesting person they are ever likely to meet.

This involves *Self Assessment.* Much more effective than any computer based profiling because it contains no *Fear Factor.*

In my opinion the power and implied potential of the computer has defeated its own purpose with psychometric profiling. Most American based systems require the participant to select one answer from a list of options in a series of probing personal questions where it becomes transparently obvious to the participant that the intention is to generate some evaluation.

Naturally, the participant will wish to convey their preferred characteristics as opposed to their true mindset, which might include a jaundiced perception of their Chief Executive. Anyone with half a brain will smart answer a psychometric test to produce their most desired reading, and this has resulted in the programmers endeavouring to outwit this reaction by devious sub-plotting which, in turn, has developed counter strategies from 'switched on' participants demanding counter-counter measures from the now demented minds of the programmers.

This circus has culminated in profiles based on preferred selection from prepared answers to questions which are so convoluted that it appears job starts, promotions and professional progress is dependent on the ability to prioritise finger nail or nose hair growth as essential elements in the human life cycle or to determine why Freds' sister had two brothers and he only had one.

The inability to determine essential facts about an individual, and their attitude to this system, has escalated into the production of what is known as 180 degree or 360 degree profiles, which in reality, means they want you to ask your family members, your friends or your work colleagues what they think of you. Pretty scientific stuff! But it is widely used because it is supplied in impressive packaging, costs a lot and therefore, by 'execu-thereof' must be good.

Personally, I am never going to give any computer information that it might regurgitate at some future date to humiliate me, embarrass me or even hang me! The information in a Self Assessment is for the participant's eyes only and should therefor be honest, accurate and, as a result, valuable.

The Most Interesting Person in the World

Make a list of the ten things which most interest you in life. *Things* being defined as people, places, activities, possessions, skills, sports, pastimes, etc.

The only qualifying essential is that every entry in your list should be interesting. *Take no more than ten minutes for this exercise.*

Consider what you have elected as the areas of life you find most interesting and then prioritise them by placing a number in each bracket being first choice. *Take no more than five minutes.*

Now list the names of ten people you know, for sure, have the exact same list of interests as you in exactly the same order of priority. *Take as long as you like for this part of the exercise.*

Unless you are a very unusual person, you will have an absolutely blank list because the odds are stacked against any two people having exactly the same interests in the same order of priority at any moment in time.

You may touch base on one or two points such as (1) My children (2) My partner (3) My home. Pretty all embracing stuff and also very likely to find replication but, as the list continues I doubt if the generalities would match and, even if they do match between you and I for instance with (1) 'My Children. ' My children are not like your children'.

Supposing 'The Car' is the third greatest interest in both your lists. Prepare a prioritised list of the ten reasons why you are so interested in the car and I absolutely *refuse to believe* you will find a perfect match with your partner.

The purpose of all this is to demonstrate to yourself that there is no other person alive; there never has been anyone who has lived; and there never will be anyone who will be exactly a match to your thought process. No living person is interested in exactly the same things as you and that, in my book, means:

You are the Most Interesting Person in the World – to You!

WISE is recognising what is CLEVER

CLEVER is knowing something and convincing others
they should pay you for what you know – That is CLEVER

WISE is knowing the value of CLEVER

We tend to find people will buy CLEVER

but seldom recognise the value of WISE

WISDOM is seldom **offered** on the open market

IT DOESN'T SELL

Evaluation?

Do you understand the intended purpose of what you have read so far?

- Was the purpose achieved?
- Was the message relevant to you?
- Can you use this information?
- Will you use this information?
- How will you use this information?
- Where and when will you use it?

Dependent on how far down that list you answered positively you should now choose from:

- Progress to the next stage
- Read the previous chapters again
- Ask someone to read the book out loud to you

CHAPTER FOUR

Men

THE MEN IN MY LIFE are all magnificent men. They have magnificent potential and they are either exciting me with their positive attitude or boosting my self esteem because I am exciting them with mine.

My pal Eddie Jackson, at Ayr's Borderline Theatre, who just recently celebrated his fiftieth birthday, went off to America to seek out the father he had never known. That must have been an incredible experience and took magnificent courage

Charles McCann of the Executive Business Services is possibly one of the sharpest financial brains in the world and lives the deserved lifestyle of a highly successful person. It would be more than acceptable for him to rest on his laurels and enjoy his earned status and wealth but he made a public declaration of a desire to create a new challenge and, in record time, achieved his helicopter pilot's license and added a new dimension to his life.

I have shared the speakers platform with Charles and know his story well, of how he crashed his car and lost his driving license along with his job as a sales rep just weeks before he was due to marry. He recognised an opportunity in the crisis and his tireless application of what is now neatly packaged as personal development, helped him to change career direction and saw him rise to the highest office in the LIA (Life Insurance Association) and the prestigious Million Dollar Round Table. His client list reads like the guest list at a premier and his reputation is revered world wide. Charles gave me a magnificent vote of approval when he took me in as a partner in the Achievement Factory. It was a short lived experience but it was the essential requirement at that point in my life and I will be eternally grateful that I have Charlie as a friend.

Other men I have shared the speakers' platform with or worked with in some capacity and drawn inspiration from would have to include Everest overlord Chris Bonnington; Rob Wainwright, captain of the Scottish rugby team; Sir Tom Farmer, founder of Kwik-Fit and the future Formula One Champion of the World,

54

This incredible piece of furniture was carved to tell the story of the man, here seen with the woman - Helen. It was crafted by the Govan chairman, John McLaughlan MBE.

The massive impact of the "Personal Enterprise Show", featured Watt Nicol and drew thousands of people wherever it appeared.

Scottish Rugby Captain, Rob Wainwright and Watt share the speakers' platform.

David Coulthard is a great example of Scottish positive motivation in action.

Watt with Owen McGee of YES and Everest overlord, Chris Bonnington.

Rhonda White of Harley Davidson has twice travelled to Scotland to work with the guru of personal re-invention.

Youngest son Rory, Watt and Gerard Kelly at showbiz ball.

Real high fliers keep their feet on the ground. Charlie McCann with the chopper.

Intimate workshops for hands-on skill transference.

Herriot Watt University lecture hall rise to the experience.

Stirling Business Links and Watt with a group preparing for the work market.

Language is no barrier to the guru of re-invention.

Working with Young Enterprise is how Watt motivates himself. Also in the group, teachers Terry Laughrin and John Collins.

International Training in Communication, World Conference, Reno, Nevada.

The magnificent Waterfront Theatre in Belfast.

Inside the Waterfront, a capacity audience enjoy the Watt Nicol experience.

David Coulthard. All of these men, and a multitude of others I have had the privilege of working with, are well recognised names and their feats are well documented but, for every one of them, I could list a thousand names you probably wouldn't recognise but are magnificent in their own special way.

My father was magnificent, proud, capable, humble and strangely protective of our family. He used to give me long lectures about the good name of the family and burden me with the responsibility of keeping it. I never had the opportunity to take him to task on this but, often when I look back on the rest of the family, I'm struggling to think of anything that was good about them other than my father. That is one of the reasons I feel my father was magnificent, because he emerged from a family who were so insipid, introverted and incapable and he broke the mould when he left his home town and raised his sights from timber conversion into management. He encouraged me to be something different and supported me in ways that must have been difficult to relate to in his own up-bringing.

I rode on the speedway at Glasgow White City for two years and at fourteen was one of the youngest novice riders, if not the youngest, in the U.K. My Dad was there and helped me buy my first bike. He found it difficult to accept my continual change of direction in educational pursuits, but even more difficulty in accepting me as an entertainer and, although I was a successful recording artiste with my own T.V. series, he would sit in the audience and wait until the audience reacted before he added his own applause. I always thought he disapproved but discovered when I spoke to his friends and the work colleagues who attended his funeral that he used to carry my LPs with him and play them everywhere he went.

One very clear memory I have of my father was as a youngster, probably aged nine or ten. I was coming down the Loons Road in Lochee, where we lived at the time, laden with two great bags of Saturday shopping. There was war time food rationing on and to get the best value for money and coupons, I was sent to queue at the Soch (Dundee Eastern Co-operative Society) whilst my mother queued at some other shop.

Money was very scarce and when entrusted with it, I was expected to account for every last half penny and every food rationing coupon. I was well aware of the financial hardships of the time and acutely aware of the great responsibility placed on me when sent on these shopping trips. I would have, I'm sure, rather died than lost a penny or a wee 'E' coupon that was so essential for the acquisition of sugar.

My father was the hirer and firer in the local sawmill and was not a man many of the others liked to tackle. I have always been convinced that when he fired anyone a large boy with brothers to back him up was given my name and I was earmarked for a beating.

I learned to protect myself with basic martial arts, like running and hiding, and normally I could just about handle these situations but, laden with two heavy bags of messages and the acute awareness of how vital my load was to the ongoing welfare of our home, I resigned myself to a beating when three adversaries suddenly appeared before me and demanded to know what was in the bags.

I couldn't run, I couldn't hide and retaliation is not a good idea when there are three against you.

I attempted to protect the family assets as blows and kicks rained in on me until I heard my Dad's voice above the sound of my own. 'Drop the bloody bags and fight back!'

I had never been given permission to fight before, even though I had heard stories of my father's prowess in that direction. I had always been punished if either parent got to know of school bashes and here I was being given full license. I'm sure it was a typical wee boys' push around, but as I choose to recall, I thrashed the three of them and absolutely revelled in my father's praise as we recounted the incident to my mother.

'Why didn't you have a go before I came on the scene,' my father asked later. I told him I was scared in case I lost any of the messages or the change. His response was one of the milestones in my own personal development:

'There comes a time in life when you have to drop other people's baggage and stand up for yourself.'

Jim McLean may be one of the most controversial of all Scottish football managers but his book 'Jousting with Giants' is one I treasure because I had the opportunity to work with the man and two of his Dundee United players Tommy Coyne and Ralph Milne. I made an agreement with Jim not to use the event for publicity and I have always honoured my agreements just as I believe he does. I will say his commitment to his goals and his belief in his people are so total that magnificent just doesn't do the man justice.

One of my very first jobs was as the Pet Man on S.T.V.s *Roundup'* programme for children with Paul Young (*Hooked on Scotland*) and Morag Hood as the young presenters and a young teacher called

Jimmy Gordon as quiz master. James Gordon is now Lord Gordon and the legend behind the Empire of Radio Clyde and another example of magnificence. When I recently interviewed him he narrowed his success down to recognition of opportunity and gave me the lovely quote:

Luck is when opportunity surpasses preparation.

I earned a living for six years within the Scottish Folk Revival and worked with many people who have achieved so much. Euro M.P. Ken Collins, Billy Connolly, Hamish Imlach and Brian Wilson the Minister of Industry who ran the Dunoon folk club as a young boy.

During that period I teamed up with John Sichell, the son of a German couple who had left their homeland in the fastest car in the world just prior to the war. John is now Principal of ARTTS International, the only professional training centre for Film and Television Directors, I believe, in the world. He directed and pro-duced the biggest and the best in the business including a long, close, and extremely successful relationship with Sir Laurence Olivier.

As writing partners, John and I sold material to the BBC, several theatre companies and ITV when we co-wrote a series for Norman Wisdom. One of the outcomes of that era was the introduction to Lionel Blair and Russell Hunter who has remained a close friend ever since and is another magnificent talent.

I have three magnificent sons Rod, Kerr and Rory who are convinced that one day they will be up there with the other great trios in history The Three Tenors or The Three Musketeers. So far I think they are modelling themselves on The Three Wise Men and relying on a miracle .

Toast and Tea is a Communication Skill

When I was very young I learned to observe the rules of the house, and these included consideration for the macho image my father insisted was observed at all times.

My Dad was a foreman at the time, the hirer and firer of men. It was not an acceptable image for such a hard-man to show open affection for his woman and he seldom ever spoke endearments or made physical contact with my mother in public.

My father was a phoney through and through in this department because when none of his work mates were around, he would hold my mother's hand or put an arm round her waist. Every night he would wait until they were alone, then he would go into the kitchen and make two cups of tea and two slices of toast, lay them out on a wee tray and take them through to my mother. That was how they finished their day.

I was never supposed to know this went on and I certainly would never have mentioned it to my Dad, but I should like to set the record straight and make sure everyone understands that he was not a total pussycat. He left the dishes for my mother to do in the morning. For twenty-five years that was how my parents ended each day and then their Silver Wedding arrived.

The event itself was a splendid occasion with every relative and friend from the past playing a significant role; the restaurant meal, the presents, the speeches and the memories relived until eventually the three of us returned home and I left them on their own and went off to the bedroom where I was spending the night.

I enjoyed the familiar sounds of the kitchen ritual and visualised the two cups of tea and the toast – even at the end of this special day where both had been wined and dined to the hilt. Tradition was what this was all about and I, once again, recognised how fortunate I was to have been born into such a stable relationship, such a solid marriage – then I heard my mother crying.

At first I put it down to emotional release before the crying intensified. I ventured down to the sitting room door, tapped and entered. 'What seems to be the problem Mum'? I enquired. 'Has the day been a wee bit too much for you'? I used the softest inflection in my voice and smiled reassuringly, but her reaction was stern, aggressive and unrelenting as she pointed at my father. 'It's him', she said accusingly, 'Every night for twenty-five years he's made me a cup of tea and a slice of toast and I've never complained once but, just this once, on such a special occasion, you would have thought he wouldn't have given me the hard end off the loaf'.

I looked at my father in disbelief as he shook his head, 'I've been giving her the hard end every night for twenty five years and that's my favourite bit'!

I ask you now, if these two people, so much in love and living under the same roof, sharing the same bed for twenty-five years, weren't communicating properly, what must communications be like in the work place with people we meet only casually?

Communicating with your fellow man/woman is obviously essential if you are to be part of any society. Even members of a silent order have means of communicating with each other and I think that many who believe themselves to be excellent communicators would be shocked if they employed a feedback system to measure how ineffectively they actually perform in this fundamental area of social interactivity.

Study of human behaviour has been conducted by many professional institutions over the years and the widely recognised facts are that people respond to information in the following manner:

55% Body Language/Facial Expressions.
8% Vocal Inflection.
7% What You Say.

Another interesting and useful study produced these figures relating to how we gather information:

87% Sight.
7% Hearing.
3.5% Smell.
1.5% Touch.
1% Taste.

I have noticed that a great many people today spend a great deal of time watching television with a remote control in their hand. This kind of power allows them to effortlessly switch from channel to channel with the least effort and absolutely no consultation with anyone. Once a person realises they have power I believe they become intolerant of that which they can change and so developed the late twentieth century social reaction I call:

Shit – Click

They sit watching TV and mentally they give the programme a few minutes attention then say, 'This is shit.' – CLICK.

Now it seems to me that, if they are doing this every night of their life, they will probably develop the habit and when you are talking to a modern day tele-chookie you had better be very interesting or, a few minutes into the conversation and they will mentally say 'This is shit' – CLICK and mentally leave your company.

One of the most effective communicators I ever knew was Hamish Imlach the legendary Scottish folk singer, guitarist and raconteur without equal.

Short in physical stature, this eighteen stone of good nature used to be introduced to audiences as the world's greatest all round entertainer and I once heard Diz Disley, in the Glasgow Folk Centre, say to an ecstatic audience demanding more of Imlach, 'That man has guts.'

It was a Saturday night and the club was virtually decked in blue as the disappointed Glasgow Rangers fans endeavoured to come to terms with the fact that they had just been dumped out of the Scottish cup by Berwick Rangers.

We had all fired our best shots but the crowd was inconsolable and, to be honest, it was not a particularly healthy atmosphere. Disley, who had regularly been voted top jazz guitarist in the world by *Melody Maker* magazine and had recently teamed up with Stephen Grappelli, was top of the bill and was, quite rightly, not too pleased at having to face the bears.

None of us fancied going back on stage but Hamish did it! He sat tuning his big Guild guitar, chuckling to himself, until one of the audience broke the silence and demanded to know what the hell he found so funny. Hamish replied instantly that he had been thinking that if the fans were taking a beating from Berwick Rangers so bad what would it have been like if they had been called Berwick Celtic. His body language, facial expression and infectious laughter defused any serious reaction and his message swept through the audience. There is nothing we can do about what is in the past so let's enjoy the present. That was Hamish's message to the world and he communicated it magnificently. Another night I remember Hamish having the unenviable task of telling a full house that the top of the bill hadn't turned up. He took it in his stride, 'Tonights' star guest needs no introduction because he's no here!'

Diz was right. Hamish had guts! Physically and mentally he paraded guts and I now understand that his stage confidence came from his communication skills. Hamish had a very expressive voice range, an infectious laugh and a great deal of body in his language. That is 93% of what people react to!

I have been asked many times why Hamish Imlach never made it as big as Billy Connolly, because Hamish was the king of the Scottish folk scene that spawned our great comedy legend. I am sure Billy will support me when I say that none of us ever got close to the reaction of an Imlach audience in these days. Well, now that I have studied the subject, and was part of the scene that they both emerged from, I know the reason why Hamish never made it as big as Billy.

Hamish didn't need much comedy material and the seven per cent in his act wasn't essential. Audiences dissolved into laughter and eagerly rushed out to share the experience with their friends and relatives only to find there was nothing to repeat.

I well remember the first time my own sons encountered Hamish when he visited our home in Bo'ness and made it impossible for them to eat their meal because they laughed so much. I heard them endeavour to extract the same response from their friends by repeating some of Hamish's stories only to be met with blank stares because there was no content. It wasn't funny without Hamish!

Billy Connolly, on the other hand, quickly learned to use body language, facial expression and vocal inflection, but the difference was he also provided the seven per cent that the poor communicators in his audience could carry away and use to good personal effect. If they told the story about the girl accepting that the love bites on her boyfriend's neck were the result of him being attacked by a gumsie alsation – their friends laughed and that made them feel good. It didn't make them a Billy Connolly but it provided immediate gratification, made them temporarily popular and legged Billy into the international stardom that eluded Hamish.

There are many speakers' clubs around the country and most of them use similar systems to encourage good communications. Each person stands up and speaks for two to three minutes and is evaluated by the others. Were you confident in your stance? Did you keep your head up? Did you fidget or play with your hands? Did you speak with a monotone and boring voice or with an attractive range of inflections? They will evaluate you on what they believe you were trying to say and whether or not you achieved this. The evaluations are usually constructive, and since everyone has the same fear factors, they tend to be supportive of each other.

I have seen massive improvement in all areas of an individual's self development as a result of regular attendance at speakers' clubs and most immediately noticeable in communications.

ITC (International Training in Communications) is the biggest of all the speakers' organisations and has the added advantage of immediately linking members with an international network of positive minded communicators, whilst organisations such as Scottish Speakers can be located locally.

Communication

What is the purpose of communication ?

Matching Human Transmitter to Human Receiver !

The Desired Outcome of Communication is to accurately pass information to or receive information from another party.

Communication barriers

Prejudice – Senior/Subordinate Relationships

Any form of prejudice or personal opinion can effectively destroy quality communication and it is fundamental to accuracy that an open mind is maintained at all times.

Language
Pre-Judgement
Differing Perceptions
Misunderstanding

Content structure

To attract and hold another persons' interest for sufficient time to impart information in sufficient detail as to effect the desired result of the communication without instigating prejudice or resistance it is necessary to:

Establish the Identity of the Sender or the Recipient
	(Dependent on which you are)
Make an Innitial Impact
Be Accurate
Be Clear, Coherent and Courteous

Speaking Skills

Thinking before speaking:
Sympathetic Pace and Tone

If you want to hold someone's attention you have to avoid any aggressive language or abrasive mannerisms and be sympathetic to their abilities as a listener i.e. There is no point whispering to someone who is deaf.

The pace and tone of voice can make all the difference when you have to communicate information the other person does not particularly want to hear i.e Laughing and throwing in one liners at someone as you tell them their granny just snuffed it would be a little insensitive.

Avoidance of Specialist Jargon

The supportive language of any specific knowledge means nothing to the average person and its' continual use only makes them feel inadequate and frustrated.

Better by far to assume they wouldn't understand and use words anyone could be expected to comprehend i.e. Pastied Marine Species with Branded Fingers of Pomme de Terre will never sell as well in Coatbridge as Fish and Chips.

Listening Skills

> Open Mindedness
> Showing Interest
> Good Powers of Concentration

Acknowledgement of Understanding

The ability to listen to everything as though it is a brand new subject to you. To give it a clear passage into your thought process as opposed to forcing it through a filter of pre-determined opinion i.e., 'I really value your opinion you bloody liar.'

If you have to listen, or you have indicated you are prepared to listen to someone, you may as well assist them to make it a worthwhile conversation and indicate interest by leaning towards them as they speak, nodding in agreement occasionally and allowing your facial expressions to change.

If you understand the point the speaker is making you should indicate this by nodding the head, repeating what they have just said in an affirmative tone or by simply saying you have got the message. Apart from bonding the two participants this could also save time.

If you don't understand the point the speaker is making you can help improve the communication by asking appropriate questions i.e. What part of BORING is it you don't understand ?

Humour Oxygenates the blood

Massages the Organs

Increases the Production of Endorphins

Laughter can increase the Effectiveness of the body's Immune System (Up to 300%)

Humour Stabilises Blood Pressure

Stimulates Circulation

Facilitates Digestion

Creates a Feeling of Well Being

Doos are No What They Used to Be

Thinking positively, we Dundonians have a decided communications advantage as we have a language only Dundonians can understand and we can indulge in conversation quite openly in the company of strangers with no fear of being understood. The broad vowel is the mainstay of our vernacular which provides dialogue such as:

'Eh'll hae a bridie.'
'Ye wanna plen ane or an ingin ane?'
'Eh'll hae a plen ane an an ingin ane anna.'

English translation:
'I would like a meat pastie.'
'Would you like a plain one or would you prefer one with onions?'
'I will have a plain one and an onion one as well.'

Speaking realistically, we Dundonians have a real communications challenge since Britain joined the Common Market. We have become European and now the business world is becoming global. Technology is taking us into, not only a new set of international relationships, but into the possibility of inter-galactic relations and, frankly, I do not really expect the Man on the Moon, if such a person exists, to understand *if we ask for a plen ane an an ingin ane anna.*

I am all for the preservation of Dundonesian and any other language that bonds people together but, unless these people also converse in a language common to the wider spectrum they will become isolated.

William Shakespeare and Robert Burns wrote some of the most acclaimed literary work in the history of mankind but the reason they are not more widely accepted by the younger generation is that their work is written in a language the majority of young people find difficult to understand. People who are attempting to communicate to a new, younger generation are relying on the content because of its acclaim and, in so doing, are only making 7% of an impression.

Dundee vernacular includes 'Eh Ken.' (I know), 'Ach awe.' (I find that hard to believe), and 'Doo' which has the duel meaning of Pigeon or Event.

Oor doos were racing pigeons and breeding these birds used to be a very popular hobby among the working classes in most

Scottish industrial areas. Doo lofts, or pigeon sheds, could be seen everywhere and most locals attended their own Doo Club.

An event such as a wedding or a funeral was also a 'doo' and would be referred to with a variety of adjectives. 'A big doo', 'a wee doo', 'a great doo', 'an awfie doo' or perhaps 'an annual doo'.

Annual doos were held by most organisations and, as a boy, I had my year scheduled in accordance with my father's 'Works doo' or the 'Boolin doo' (Bowling Club Prize Presentation), 'Darts doo' or, the biggest event of the year – The 'Doo doo'. You would be forgiven for being confused if I were to tell you that my father and his cronies were regularly Flee'n at the Doo doo, not because they were pigeons, but because they were alcoholically inebriated. You see, we in Dundee instantly knew what had happened when we heard somebody had been 'flee'n at the Doo doo' but I doubt very much if the rest of the world would have known and, *so long as we continued to talk like that, I doubt if the rest of the world would have cared.*

A very important lesson I have learned in life is that progress is seldom made without good communications with other people and to do this we have to avoid specialist or jargon talk that others cannot understand.

I recall shopping for my first computer when I was fifty-five. The shop assistant used words like bytes and ROM's and baffled me with techno-talk. I wanted to buy the computer but I was obliged to protect my self esteem and reacted by pretending to understand with a mirroring technique.

If the assistant said the machine had a certain feature I would feign knowledge and answer, 'Since when?' This technique can elevate your credibility for a short time when you are out of your depth but I eventually blew my cover when he told me the PC was 64K and I countered by saying I doubted if it would ever sell at that price. The result of the experience was that the young salesman didn't make his commission and I didn't get my computer. He needed that specialist jargon to communicate with his own kind but he should have realised not everyone was as well informed as himself.

My mother used to tell me that if I found myself out of my depth in company I should always fall back on the *golden rule*:, 'Do unto others as you would have them do unto you.'

It seemed I could never go wrong with the *golden rule* and if I spoke to people as I liked to be spoken to I could pay them no greater compliment.

Remember – I was born and raised in Dundee. I liked to be spoken to in Dundonesian. – 'Ken whit e'm tellin yu?'

When I worked with the Italia Conti Drama School do you think I would have acquitted myself well had I spoken to them as I liked to be spoken to?

My mother proved the Golden Rule doesn't work. She loved to talk. My Mum would talk to anyone about anything at anytime, whether they wanted to or not. My Mum could have talked for Scotland and, because she liked to hear other people's thoughts and experiences, she assumed everyone else felt the same and she applied the Golden Rule and told everyone her thoughts and experiences. I best remember her in a Dundee restaurant when it was her birthday and she engaged one of the diners in her kind of communication which went something like:

'Are you here for anything special?'

'Your birthday. That's nice. How old are you?'

'Forty nine!' (In a voice raised to allow all other diners to share this very interesting piece of information)

'What do you do for a living?'

'You sell insurance! Do you make a good living at that'?

Although the man on the other end of the dialogue was becoming increasingly uncomfortable, my mother was totally oblivious of this and most of the other diners were by now mildly interested to know the answer to her next question. 'How much do you make'?

At this point she would realise that her rule was bearing no fruit and probably disqualified the male for that very reason – Men are not good conversationalists. That was something she was very sure of and an opinion she often aired. On this occasion she turned her attention to the mans' partner and, conspiratorially, asked in a very loud whisper:

'I notice your friend is wearing a wedding ring and you are not. Would you like to talk about that?' The tone of her voice was considerably more sympathetic than the reaction of her victims but everyone in that restaurant was extremely interested and, although the purpose of my mothers' conversation was the application of the golden rule and she was doing unto these people as she would have liked to have been done unto, that is some interest shown in her life, I doubt if that couple ever looked back on that birthday celebration as the night they met that very friendly lady.

The *golden rule* does not apply to communication and you should not do unto others as you would have them do unto you. In my opinion this means you are giving no consideration as to how others would like to be treated and the Platinum Rule must be 'Do unto others as they would like to be done unto.'

Don't ever ignore more traditional methods of personal development. Asking your parents or grandparents for advice can often be very helpful. I once asked my father what I should do after receiving a prize at the forthcoming Boys Brigade Presentation. His advice?

'You've seen what happens at our social events. Just do whit eh do at the doo doo!'

Stand up and speak out

'It's not what you do it's how you do it' – RIGHT
'It's not what you know it's who knows you ' – RIGHT
'It's not what you say it's how you say it' – BETTER BELIEVE IT!

Whether you have that once in a lifetime speech as the best man or the prize giving acceptance speech at the tennis club or you require speaking skills to enhance your career. Learn to prepare speech materials, speak confidently, listen effectively and make quality communication either for personal or professional use and you will multiply your personal ability in all fields by 'loadsa'.

The *ability to stand up and clearly express yourself* can determine how successful you are in life. Politicians rise to prominence or fade to insignificance on the strength of how they express themselves, Lawyers win or lose court cases not so often on what they say, but rather on how they say it.

Business relationships, personal relationships, love affairs and families thrive or writhe dependent on the ability of those involved to impart what they really feel.

Many organisations and scientific schools have conducted research into Human Fear Factors and always with a somewhat pre-dictable list of Spiders and being Buried Alive. Just death, in its' most natural form, is fifth in the overall league of fears, whilst first, the number one greatest fear of modem mankind is standing up and speaking publicly.

This translates into the simple fact that most people would rather be burnt to death with spiders crawling all over them, buried alive or kiss a toad than stand up in public and say something.

Perception has a great deal to do with this. How you see others when they speak and what you think of them as a result of your observations determines what you assume others will think of you when you speak. I only recently experienced unexpected resistance from the executive level of a large organisation in spite of having effectively brought about massive improvement in the overall performance of their entire work force.

My initial reaction was surprise, my next reaction was curiosity and then amusement when it was eventually disclosed that my motivational methods had aroused the interest of the chairman who disapproved of and mistrusted people with beards.

Well I never did get the opportunity to discuss this further with the gentleman but I guarantee his ridiculous attitude had some deep rooted origin based on someone sporting a beard who had wronged him in the past and that concerns me ever so slightly when you consider all of us have to come to terms with the Santa Clause disappointment at some point in our life .

There is a very definite case for the belief that we become whatever we think about and most of us have experienced the childhood thought that there was a monster in the bedroom or perhaps that the boss didn't like us.

You dwell on something and eventually, sure as God made sour wee green apples, it becomes reality. Nobody else could see that monster but you just knew that it was there and, whilst everybody tells you very convincing reasons why the boss has the greatest respect for you, - you just know that he really is biding his time to boot you.

If you give more emphasis to your memories of people making total clicks of themselves by standing up to thank the President of the Bowling Club for the kind remarks he made, drying up and shaking like a leaf, nervously lifting a glass of water to moisten their mouth then realising they've just swallowed the Lord Provosts' gin, attempting to make a joke of it, belching and then barfing on the table, then the chances are that this will become your anticipated outcome of any effort you might be tempted to make and you will generate an incredible resistance to speaking publicly.

If you literally become what you think about there would be a great deal of senior executives change into large brandies and fat slobs would all become Pizzas or Burgers.

When you get right down to it, if you became what you predominantly think about, the majority of men would become women and quite a few ladies would become men, but then, now that I contemplate that area and survey todays' society, maybe we do become what we think about after all.

Think about the many public speakers you have admired, possibly even been thrilled by Think of the effect the character of William Wallace had when he made his motivational speech to the clansmen in the Braveheart movie. Think of some of the great orators through the centuries like Winston Churchill, Martin Luther King, Billy Graham and Hosie Broon.

These people could inspire and motivate others. They could virtually create their own world whilst they were on that platform and, in sharing their vision, they could enhance the lives of all around them.

Now it may be that all you want to do is speak up for yourself. You want to get a better job or promotion. You want to raise a loan to start a business.

It may be that what you have to do is an every day sale of yourself, or some service or product, but, whether it is a once only or an essential every day part of your life, if you dwell on your perception of a good speaker and allow yourself to relive the experience, you will develop a desire to be like them and:

desire leads to action!

Just as people learn to drive, ride a bicycle, swim or play a musical instrument, you can learn how to speak. It simply requires a recognition of the need, a commitment to improvement and you can enhance your private life and add to your professional skills as a regular speaker, presenter or sales person.

It has just occurred to me that you may be curious as to who Hosie Broon was. He was my uncle and could sell snow to the eskimos!

Vocabulary which is totally negative

When you are writing a speech, making a presentation or communicating by either spoken or written word, avoid the use of negative terms. Equally be prepared to counter negative vocabulary which can be very de-motivating.

Who do you know who uses some of the following?

We've never done it that way before

It wont' work

We haven't time

It's not in the budget

We've tried that before

All right in theory but . . .

It's against our policy

Too much paperwork

Let's not step on anybodys' toes

Too futuristic

Too old fashioned

Why change something at this stage ?

Why start something new ?

We have too many projects now

Has anyone else ever tried this ?

Let's do some research and then have another meeting

Let's be practical

Let's form a committee

Vocabulary which gets things done

I agree

That's good

That's a great idea

I have faith in you

See, you can do it

Let's be the first to do it

Let's start a new trend

I know it will work

We can do a lot with this idea

I like it

Go ahead – try it

It's my decision

I made a mistake – I'm sorry (end of story)

Beautiful Motivated Dreamer

Motivation is a very personal thing. I find that people who can motivate themselves in any situation and against all odds are people who know what they want.

Motivation is activating a mental button which produces maximum focus, the very ultimate determination to reach your goal. When you visualise your most passionate dream, it makes you think positively about what you really, really want.

It is exciting to realise that you don't need to win the lottery to enjoy a successful future. You can have anything you want if:

(A) you know **what *you*** want and (B) *you* want it bad enough.

I often ask people in my development workshops and seminars what they really want and I seldom get a definite response. Usually it comes down to money in some shape or form and I have no truck with that at all because, although I am not motivated by the thought of a personal fortune, I do have my standards and I've found that if I pay my bills, life tends to go a little smoother. We all need finance and if you think of it as Financial Freedom rather than Wealth that would mean having enough money to never have to worry about money.

Make a list of all the things you want in life, then prioritise them. Starting your own business may embrace other items on your list such as independence, financial freedom, the opportunity to travel, etc. etc.

Once you have established your number one desire in life, keep asking yourself why you want it and keep writing down the answers. These are the affirmations that will motivate you.

Life, like all modes of travel, requires either an engine or an understanding of nature, otherwise you end up at the mercy of the elements.

If you have been blown about a bit and feel all washed up and a bit like a beached whale you have two options. Come to terms with your lot and make the best of it, much like a yachtsman dealing with a storm, or kick start your engine and get the hell out of it with some idea of where you are going, with plenty fuel and good steering gear to make sure you get there.

Motivation is an Internal Combustion Engine requiring Fuel and Spark.
It can be fuelled by ambition, jealousy, success, hatred or failure.
It can be sparked by a desire, a compliment or even a thought.

Steering Gear: A Carefully constructed Plan.
        (Requires Quality Goal Setting)

Fuel: Passion for the outcome of the Plan.
        (Something you really want to do)
        (Continually Visualising the Feel Good Factor)

Spark: A Surge of Immediacy.

Spaghetti and Rhubarb

Spaghetti and Rhubarb sounds like a horrendous mixture when first contemplated because it is immediately visualised on the same plate, but, in the hands of a capable cook, more than acceptable on the same menu.

The LEFT BRAIN/RIGHT BRAIN function may be understood by many people but few recognise what a full understanding of 'Why we have developed Left Hemispherical Dominance' can lead to.

Recognition of awesome personal abilities

It can empower the individual to release lateral thinking skills and originality.

Effective and positive attitude towards academic study.

Remove negative limitations.

The academic explanation of the LEFT BRAIN/RIGHT BRAIN control can be a very involved study and I am first to admit that I have never cut the top off another persons' head and had a look for myself but I can give you the benefit of all my reading and study of the subject, which breaks down into the following explanation.

The inventive and original right brain is unreasonable and impractical. It is where we fantasise and dream and is the origin of our creativity which is the major difference between man and most of the other species on earth.

The logistic and factual left brain contains the memory and all its limiting self beliefs. Because it contains the memory it contains our education and our experiences, both good and bad.

To be dominated by either is obviously mentally restricting but is commonly recognised as the only practical application. Poets, artistes, writers and other creative pusuants are usually Right Brain Dominant whilst the more conventional and logistic members of society are generally Left Brain Dominant.

Accountants are Left Brain Dominant because they are working within logistic disciplines. Architects are Right Brain dominant because they are required to be inventive and are often, as a result, perceived by accountants as impractical.

Accountants and Architects often have difficulty in relating to each other,

One seeking to produce something which has original creative content whilst the other works within the present reality of costs and viability.

LEFT BRAIN dominance is essential for the practical support of discipline whilst RIGHT BRAIN Activity is the essential source of progress. Like spaghetti and rhubarb, they do not appear to have a great deal in common but if they are managed by a whole brain thinker, the benefits of both can be appreciated and enjoyed to the full on the same menu.

Now I would encourage you to employ your left brain memory in a little time travel and try to recall when you had an idea that seemed to be really worthwhile but you took no action on it and now, when you recall it, your thought process went something like this.

LEFT BRAIN   **RIGHT BRAIN**

Careful now. Maybe your friends just say they like your cakes and really think they're nothing special.
Anyway. It would take up all your spare time and the family would suffer.

I'm a pretty good baker. Everybody seems to like my cakes. Why don't I supply some of the local tea rooms with my home bakery goods?

If you get started on something like that you'll end up working day and night on it and your marriage will suffer. You know how he is about a woman's place being in the home.
If any of the children overheard anybody saying something bad about the tea room you supplied they would be embarrassed.

I could always just try it out and if I got a return order I would know they liked my stuff. The extra money could finance a holiday or maybe a second car for taking the children to school.

There you go already. Just thinking about selling a few fancy cakes and you're already planning the interior design for a national chain of restaurants. If that was what you wanted out of life you should never have got married. Never had children.

And if it all failed? Have you considered how that would effect the family, marriage and your self respect in this area?

I could allocate certain times of the day for baking and I don't have to even tell the children where I'm selling my stuff.

This could build up and someday I could even open my own tea room.

This mental exercise is called Self Talk and it is something we all indulge in. It protects us from our impetuous desires and is the very core of all self discipline but it generates Left Brain dominance and invariably means that, once we have found a lifestyle which is reasonable, we resist any thoughts of changing our lot because we listen to the 'Self Limiting" council of the Left Brain.

Comfort Zone survival is Left Brain living

Right Brain dominance is always a risk because it inviariably means trying something different, something new, something you have never done before. It can be an exciting thought but it can lead to disastrous results.

Quality use of your thinking processes would be the use of the Left Brain to evaluate the produce of the Right Brain but to extend the Left Brain activity to secondary evaluation of the origin of the 'Self Limiting' beliefs. Challenge them and, where possible, eliminate them. Now you are employing Whole Brain thinking and here are the mechanics of the process.

Consider the two sides of the brain as a couple who are sharing a flat. Both have their individual characteristics and both have a recognition of the need for the other.

This is a positive start to a relationship but, as time wears on, one of the partners develops a superior attitude based on having been proven right in a number of disputes. Peace is usually maintained when one partner, in such a situation concedes to the superiority of the other and, when it comes to decisions, an acceptable code is established where they both make suggestions and observations but final decisions are left to the one who has the track record.

Both partners are very comfortable with this and it is obviously preferable to continual dispute which would eventually destroy the relationship. However, one day the less dominant partner decides to do something which is very important to them and they defy the reason and the objections of the other partner who realises, eventually, that this decision is of major importance to the other person and that they are hell bent on doing it and, if they want this relationship, which has been so good for so long, to continue, they will not only have to agree to the other person doing it but will also have to support them and bring to that support all the benefits of their superior knowledge. Working together, as a team, instead of bickering over their difference of opinion is very likely to bring about a desired result.

Ninety nine per cent of the time, your Right Brain concedes to the Left Brain because the brain essentially requires agreement between the two hemispheres, otherwise something happens when neither half concedes that we perceive as a kind of madness.

All of us experience temporary madness at some point when we desperately want something but realise it is totally impractical. We try to hang on to the possibility knowing the probability is negative.

Now, knowing that one will concede to the other and having a Big Dream – Target – Goal – Desired Outcome and resisting all of your Self Limiting Beliefs – something quite magical happens and the Left Brain starts to support the desires of the Right Brain.

As the Left Brain contains all your experiences in life, all your education and all your personal mental skills and the mechanism of the brain is anxious to re-establish a good relationship between the two sides – the whole brain starts to really function, to dig deeper and find answers. Your ability to think, reason, calculate and effectively plan for the successful outcome of your goal becomes awesome and that is the thinking process of a successful person.

If I travel back in time, I can remember a Left Brain / Right Brain dispute when I was fourteen years old and fell in love for the first time. She was beautiful in my eyes and I wanted to spend the rest of my life making her happy. I could not sleep at night. My Right Brain was on fire as I imagined the quality of life I could experience shared with this gorgeous female creature. My Right Brain tormented me and I became deaf to the Left Brain. I was experiencing Temporary Madness until lack of sleep weakened me and, after four days and nights of torture, I heard this other voice, this voice of reason in my head saying we needed sleep.

The voice explained the reason for analysing the situation and patiently explained that the love affair could never blossom because she was my maths teacher, was married and was probably at least three times my age. Begrudgingly my Right Brain conceded to the Left, we slept and harmony was restored.

Evaluation is simply a measure of added value

Do you understand the intended purpose of what you have read so far?

- Was the purpose achieved?
- Was the message relevant to you?
- Can you use this information?
- Will you use this information?
- How will you use this information?
- Where and when will you use it?

Dependent on how far down that list you answered positively you should now choose from:

- Progress to the next stage
- Read the previous stage again
- Try to think creatively, resist logic and invent some alternative use for the book.

CHAPTER FIVE

You can have a body like mine in ten days

THE ADVERTISEMENTS FOR Charles Atlas's bodybuilding courses were everywhere when I was a boy. They appeared in national newspapers, magazines, comics etc. and excited and inflamed the imaginations of young boys and grown men throughout the world. They always depicted a pathetic seven stone weakling with a beautiful girl sitting on the beach and some muscle-bound bully humiliating the wimp by kicking sand in his face. As a 'class A' physical wimp, I always read the advert. I knew the story in infinite detail but I still read it every time I saw it because I didn't like being a wimp and Charles Atlas offered a solution.

Atlas, a blond-headed Adonis, was featured in the accompanying photograph with a speech bubble, which said, 'I Charles Atlas, can make you a fine example of Vibrant Manhood in only 15 Minutes a Day"

He went on to explain that he had been a 97-pound runt until he discovered DYNAMIC TENSION and now he was a multi-millionaire who enjoyed being besieged by gorgeous females and he was prepared to share his secrets with you for a small fee.

There were a multitude of reasons why I was so attracted to that advert and much of my work can now relate to some of the lessons I learned from the Charles Atlas marketing strategies. That name for a start – Charles Atlas. Doesn't that just tell you exactly what the guy was all about? Like Appollo Creed from the first Rocky movie. A name that perfectly describes the world heavyweight boxing champion.

The first thing I remember about the Charles Atlas adverts was that, in spite of my fascination with the concept of Dynamic Tension, I didn't send off for the free information pack and I have to ask myself why? It seemed a great opportunity and I really fancied being besieged by gorgeous women. I now know that dreaming is just a pleasant pastime and only becomes constructive when it evolves into the motivated action that can convert it into reality.

I think the advert intrigued me but didn't convince me because, in the North-East of Scotland we didn't spend much time on beaches and, even in mid summer, you wear two jumpers and a donkey jacket and spend most of your time trying to keep your condensed milk sandwich out of the sand blowing in the wind.

Nobody could tell if you were a 'runt' or not because we all looked like cricket umpires or a wino that had fallen into the skip at the back of the Oxfam shop and there were seldom any women to impress. I think they stayed away from the beach because in these days girls didn't have donkey jackets. Even on a cracking day when the sun was shining and you stripped down to your world war two swimming costume, the wind was so cold off the North Sea that you wore a plastic mac on top. What Charles Atlas was selling was practical, usable, effective and instantly understandable in America but Broughty Ferry, Carnoustie and even Arbroath – a different story.

Arbroath did produce a powerful association with Charles Atlas in the person of Graham Brown. I first met Graham at Grampian T.V., where I presented many a programme and on this occasion it was 'Bothy Nichts' which was, in my opinion, the fore runner to all the soaps and was based on the rural lifestyle of the North-East of Scotland. Graham Brown was a professional strongman and we formed a great friendship and toured together in many shows. I wrote and recorded 'The Ballad of Graham Brown' to celebrate him setting a world record for breaking six inch nails and eventually eeked the secret of his strength and physique from him during a memorable late night bletheraganza. Graham Brown, big strong man free Arbroath town, had been a wimp and had sent for the Charles Atlas Dynamic Tension Course. My God – It works! I pleaded for information. I begged for guidance and I started calculating how many gorgeous women I really wanted to attract. I started making mental lists of arses I wanted to kick.

The first piece of information required no apparatus whatsoever and I broke all personal mental records as I processed my dreams through thoughts, visualisation and an action plan. The following morning I arose ready for action.

Every morning, Graham informed me, he filled a basin with ice cold water, squatted naked over this receptacle and carefully lowered his testicles into it. This simple process apparently had multudious effects on the masculine functions and set a man up for the day. I have only ever performed this ritual once and therefore am no expert but the pain and the anguish I experienced over the next five hours before my testicles reappeared gave me an insight into why people like Charles Atlas and Graham Brown tore up telephone directories. I tore paper off the walls, linoleum off the floor and doors off their hinges.

I now know that the real secret of Dynamic Tension has little to do with any secret or expensive apparatus. It is the determination to achieve results, the ability to persist when the pain starts, the patience and understanding to accept that it takes time and there is no magic button or instant result whilst the most important part of all is the self discipline to do fifteen minutes every day and that means every single day.

What Graham Brown taught me was that he had the physique I wanted just because he wanted it more than me. I thought about it and fancied it if it was instant. He wanted it enough to work for it over a sustained period of time.

What the Charles Atlas marketing recognised all these years ago was:

What attracts people to effectively change for the better is recognition of their present circumstances and the fact that there is a means of enhancing them.

Personal improvement means changing your habits by persistent and repetitive practice of your new preferred behaviour (routine?).

Why all men in the U.K. do not have a Charles Atlas physique.

What works for Americans in America doesn't necessarily work for Scots in Scotland.

You have to believe in Oz to follow the Yellow Brick Road.

A typical Charles Atlas ad of the time. This was the man who commercially introduced personal development to the world of young men who had never previously considered that the physical could be attained through employment of the mental. That brawn indeed could be the product of brain!

Time Management / Values

Time is Money. But unlike money, which can be made and lost and made again, time wasted can never be made up or recovered.

Time is much more valuable than money, but to give some indication of time value relative to money, try this exercise:

The Value of Time

Example:

> Based on there being 168 hours in a seven day week.
>
> Weekly salary divided by 168 = Personal Monetary Value i.e.
>
> £200 per week divided by 168 = £1.19 per hour.
>
> Personal Value on the life market is £1 .19 per hour.
>
> Time spent watching television or reading a book costs this person £1.19 per hour
>
> Sleep (8 hours per night) 56 h.p.w. = £66.64 (weekly cost of sleeping)
>
> Personal Maintenance 1.5 hours per day = 10.5 h.p.w. = £12.49
>
> (cost of dressing/undressing etc.)
>
> Work (8 hours/5 days) = 40 h.p.w. = £47.60
>
> (cost of investment in work)
>
> Eating (1.5 hour per day) = 10.5 h.p.w. = £12.49
>
> (cost of eating time.)
>
> Leaves a total of 51 hours per week valued at £1. 19 per hour.

This is all you have to invest in your quest for achievement and that is after you spend some of this time on things such as: Social Activities, Family, Housekeeping, Car Maintenance, House Maintenance etc.

We all accept the practice of placing a financial value only on income relative to work hours but if you offset everything you earn in an average week against seven twenty four hour days you get some way of measuring the financial cost of living.

I emphasise that I do not value life only in monetary terms but I am seeking here to alert the reader to some understanding of just exactly what the relative value of time spent on improving life through study, exercise or extra work is against the cost of, for instance, aimlessly watching television.

The Greatest Investment of All

Time Spent on Maximising Potential

Observe from the given example that the investment into work time was £47.60 for a return of £200. This is a sound investment showing a considerable profit by our system of measurement.

Consider now someone with this Lifetime Value of £1.19 per hour and they watch television twenty hours every week. In five weeks they have invested 100 hours at £1.19, making a total investment of £119. Ask yourself what kind of return they can expect for their investment.

Once you calculate your own Time Value you will be in a position to overview time in the same manner as a Financial Broker would plan his investments. I suggest that the above example would stand eight hours per week study, which would cost £9.52, but could perhaps lead to a qualification and an improved position in the workplace with the accompanying salary raised by possibly another £50 per week, showing a massive return for a small investment.

Time is the Stuff Your Life is Made of

The Value of Your Life

Get to know your own Lifetime Value as a way of measuring your time investments.

Understand the difference between:

Investing your time

Spending your time

Squandering your time

Gambling your time

Wasting your time

What is your average net earnings per week?

Divide the answer by 168 to establish your personal time value.

How many hours do you sleep in the average week?

How many hours do you spend on personal maintenance? (Dressing/ Bathing etc.) in an average week?

How many hours do you work in an average week?

How many hours do you spend eating per week?

Other areas of your time schedule you might wish to evaluate for consideration could include:

Social Activities

House Maintenance

Car Maintenance

Family

Shopping

Watching TV

Multiply your hourly value by hours spent in any area to establish the costs!

Once you evaluate the cost of time and recognise the massive loss with absolutely to return or justification, you tend to become very time conscious for a while until you readjust and then, as though a miracle has occurred, you suddenly find you have time for yourself.

Most people I take through time study are shocked at how little time they spend doing things for themselves or things they enjoy doing (enhanced minutes). Becoming time aware leads to becoming time effective and ultimately time rich.

TIME TO YOURSELF !

How to Cut out Time Wasters

For the Boss

Get an assistant to deal with time wasters.

Say *no* more often (politely).

Draw up a list of people you would and another list of those you would not be prepared to speak to and give it to your staff.

If you have urgent paperwork etc. to do, move into another room where you would not be expected to be (only your PA knows you're there).

Make it clear to sales reps you only see them by appointment.

Encourage staff to solve problems for themselves by suggesting that they don't bring problems to you without also providing their own suggestions.

> *Don't' tell me your problems, show me your progress*
>
> John Sichell

When you delegate work, explain the desired outcome. Encourage them to reach that stage by whatever means they are capable of.

Avoid chit-chat during conversation. Polite chit chat at the outset of conversation is easiest to cut short.

Have certain times of the day when you just do not take any calls.

Develop a phrase that indicates your time is limited i.e.

> *'I'm afraid this will have to be brief.'*
>
> *'I'm due at another meeting in twenty minutes.'*
>
> *'Have to be on hand for an international call.'*

If you have a meeting with a known time expander, arrange for someone to phone you at a given time.

Don't attend any meetings unless the outcome affects you directly or you have specific input.

Decline to sit on committees unless they are essential to your work, you enjoy them or they are profitable.

Instead of replying to a letter or memo by typing a response, simply jot a hand written reply on the original and fax backto the sender.

Try not to travel to a meeting if a phone call would suffice.

If an out of office meeting involves four people or less consider tele-conferencing.

Have your name removed from the circulation lists of unnecessary magazines and other printed material.

If you have to read a long document, skim over it and high light words or sentences that you might consider important. It will be easier to re-read and refer to later.

Let your policy be Do IT Now , but always prioritise.

If you keep putting off a task, stop and ask yourself if it is really necessary anyway.

Break long and heavy projects into chunks and do something pleasant between them.

Use the wastepaper bin.

Keep a To Do list before you at all times.

Use train or air travel to catch up on reading.

Use car travel to listen to tapes. Members of staff, etc., can read material onto a cassette and then you can listen to it as you drive.

Eat small meals several times a day and take an occasional walk. This helps concentration.

Take time to relax for a few minutes, even on the busiest of days. Trying to rush something can lead to expensive mistakes.

When delegated work is completed satisfactorily, be sure to thank the person responsible enthusiastically. It makes them more receptive to your next request.

Want to try another Evaluation?

Do you understand the intended purpose of what you have read so far?

- Was the purpose achieved?
- Was the message relevant to you?
- Can you use this information?
- Will you use this information?
- How will you use this information?
- Where and when will you use it?

Dependent on how far down that list you answered positively you should now choose from:

- Progress to the next stage
- Read the previous chapters again
- Take some time to think about it

CHAPTER SIX

Attitude

P ERSONAL DEVELOPMENT is your purpose for being in this life. Anytime you look around and wonder what this life is all about, every single time you consider the schedule of challenges that lie ahead of you and ask yourself that perennial question; 'What is it all about? What is the purpose of being here?' Consider that you were introduced to this life as a baby with no self concept, no preconception, no self esteem, no apparent purpose other than survival.

It is your experiences that create self-concept, and it is your estimation of your personal experiences, at any given point of the journey, that determines your attitude and your direction for the next stage.

Everyone has potential to some degree and everyone has the ability to develop it, to maximise their potential, to be everything they are capable of being. This is within the reach of every single one of us.

It is not the right, the domain or the responsibility of our parents, our teachers, our government or any other person or group.

It is a personal thing, controlled and powered from within each and every one of us, and it is called Personal Development.

The reason it is not developed by everyone is because of negative attitude.

If you accept that a baby is born with no self-concept and then builds that concept through life experience and you accept that the eventual self-concept of all human beings, geniuses, idiots, me, and most important of all, you, consists of three components:

INHERITED ATTRIBUTES

ACQUIRED ATTRIBUTES

ATTITUDE

Furthermore, the sum of all that you inherited, your bone structure to your I.Q., and all you acquired such as your education, skills etc., is, at best, fifteen per cent of your self concept, then you must accept that attitude is eighty-five per cent of what you really are.

Success in this life is not about wealth, good looks, skills, power or any other of the many misconceptions. Being a success is being the best you can possibly be and that means developing everything you have going for you.

The first thing to develop is a desire for development. Once you desire it, your attitude changes, and once that happens you recognise that attitude is a controllable factor.

ATTITUDE is simply a degree of determination

The longer you live the more you realise the effect ATTITUDE has had on your life.

ATTITUDE, to me, is the most important component of any individual or group of people.

ATTITUDE is more important than anything that has ever happened in the history of mankind, more important than money, success or failure, education or what somebody else thinks about you.

ATTITUDE is more important than good looks, talent or intelligence.

ATTITUDE can destroy a home, a family, an organisation, a team, an individual or a belief.

ATTITUDE is the most powerful weapon in the human mental arson. It comes in many Forms – POSITIVE–NEGATIVE–INDIFFERENCE and it comes in a range of intensities and every single moment of every single day every single one of us has the ability to select which ATTITUDE we will use.

We are incapable of changing facts, of controlling elements or turning back time. We are powerless against the inevitable and always at the mercy of others' opinions and deeds, but we can counter anything with the right ATTITUDE.

The Black Abbot

Let me introduce you to a Scottish character I long since realised was responsible for the majority of negative acceptance and probably the greatest counter force to motivation North of the Borders. I call this character THE BLACK ABBOT.

The Black Abbot is the defender of the Scotsman's right to be depressed if he wants to be. The Black Abbot raises his voice in all walks and is a powerful orator. You will hear him speak through the voice of friends, colleagues, children, employees, bank managers and traffic wardens, all of whom react to any positive suggestion or optimism with these two Scottish words of woe, 'Ah but.'

Kill the habit, destroy the Abbot and you become the programmer of the ultimate computer. The *nap top* below your hat that develops your potential to the full, plans your life, solves problems, makes decisions, manages time and ultimately takes you to your goal.

When you accept that the genius is credited with making practical use of no more than two and a half per cent of their brain power, you realise that the idiot has sufficient brain power to overwhelm the most advanced computer technology known to modern man.

In this society you do not ever get what you want but you can depend on getting what you expect. This area between what you want and what you expect is an area you have to develop. You have to develop techniques and skills to bridge the gap between what you want, what you dream of having or being, and the present reality, with its cold hard facts establishing what you can expect.

This bridge is called the Personal Development Plan and can provide you ultimately with everything you want. In the field of Personal Development I truly believe that: *If anybody has what you want, they just wanted it more than you.* Personal Development costs nothing, can be learned anywhere and practised wherever you are. It is, if you like, mental training, and everyone of us carries our own, fully equipped, mental gym around with us. You have the ability to weld what you want into what you expect, making what you want and what you expect one and the same thing, and, in this life, you invariably get what you expect, therefore, you end up getting what you want. You can have anything or be anything you expect. You have the ability, all you have to do is develop it.

You instantly understand and accept the word development in connection with career, education or perhaps even personal relationship. It is instantly acceptable that, if you wish to get the best out of a marriage or a relationship, both partners must develop skills in understanding, co-operation, supportive behaviour etc. etc. The promotion to supervisor of a small department takes on a different significance if it is understood that the department is to be developed into an independent, free standing, company and, providing you can develop along with it, there is the possibility you will be the executive figure in this new company. Young, raw, footballing talent is tolerated within the most sophisticated teams because, it is hoped, it will develop.

Planning and building development throughout the country is an everyday fact of life so it would be reasonable to say that we are all familiar with both the need for and the purpose of development in every aspect.

Let me now question what happens when some town or county planning project doesn't develop or ponder over the most likely fate of a company who did not develop any new products. What happens within a marriage when the two partners do not develop a respect for each other?

Without development, nothing ever reaches a desired outcome.

The dream may be there, the vision, the goal if you like, and the plan carefully constructed, but development means change. To change for the better. To change present reality to a new desirable outcome.

Incremented development, inch by inch, step by step, day by day, ever changing, moving closer and closer, developing shape, reforming, increasing impetus and establishing purpose is all around us. Change is all around us. The world is changing faster now than ever before because of technology. Global factors have an instant effect on domestic conditions and individual opinion can have catastrophic effect globally within seconds because of the development of communications.

Never before has there been such instant evidence of the theory of universal law. Somewhere in Brazil a butterfly spreads its wings and there is an avalanche in Nebraska.

So, as the world develops, everything in it must also develop or become obsolete. People engineered most of these developments and yet people are the most significant victims of the changes. It is becoming abundantly clear that new global developments provide little solace for those who embrace traditional ways.

The new world offers, however, unabounding opportunities for those who develop within the changes and unbelievable heights for those who are courageous enough to make the changes. Leadership and Change are two words you will find on the same page of the new world dictionary as Development.

The Mental Gymnasium

Consider the word gymnasium in a more familiar application : *The Physical Gymnasium.*

You would hardly believe me if I claimed that, by spending three hours in a gym lifting weights and pedalling a stationary bicycle, you could effectively change your body shape and acquire instant physical fitness.

You would, however, be more inclined to accept that regular visits to the gym and regular exercise would, over a period of time, effectively improve your physical fitness and enhance your general well being. *The Mental Gymnasium is no different.*

Your self esteem, attitude control, discipline in areas of time and relationships, belief in your abilities to communicate, further educate and maximise your potential are all dependent on regular exercise within, what I refer to as, the Mental Gymnasium.

What is happening as you read is by way of introducing you to the available facilities within this exclusive campus. I say exclusive because it is truly customised to each and every one of your individual needs and is immediately available, totally portable, and absolutely free.

The Mental Gymnasium is carried like a headtop computer wherever you go. Once you become familiar with its use, can also be instantly and secretly converted into a silent, invisible, dedicated back-up service capable of recognising, analysing, prioritising and maximising advantage whilst dealing with feeling and coping with stress.

Ah but! The full effectiveness of the gym can only be appreciated and its benefits enjoyed if it is visited regularly over a period of time.

Just like the physical gym, the ultimate results will take time but, unlike the iron pumpers, the mental gymnasts also have this immediate freedom of access and will recognise the improvement from the immediate outset. Typical mental gymnasium exercises would be problem solving and decision making.

Problem Solving can be categorised

Reliable information determines whether or not it is a problem.

Determine whether or not it is actually your problem.

Make a decision and take action.

Making a decision

Every day and in every way everyone lives by multiples of decisions. From you open your eyes you decide when to rise, what to wear, what to eat, where to go, when to leave, what to say etc. etc.

Most of these decisions are not life changing or threatening and should be afforded minimum consideration Tea or Coffee ?

Sugar ? Milk ? All of these are decisions but they are: PARAMETER DECISIONS.

More meaningful decisions fall into two main categories POLICY and ANALYSES.

POLICY DECISIONS are decisions that have to be made, if not regularly, at least repetitiously over a period of time. They are very important and can be life changing or controlling i.e.:

> I will not drive when I am drinking !

> I always buy British manufactured when it is available !

> I never mix business with pleasure !

A policy decision is arrived at by sourcing all the information on any subject, analysing it, emotionalising it, working through all scenarios and a gradual process of elimination until a clear decision is made and never requires a second thought when it arises in some other shape or form. i.e. If you were buying a washing machine and went through this process, arriving at the decision that buying British promoted economy in your own society, that would be a policy decision that would save time when you were deciding on a car.

An ANALYSES is a different type of decision because it is non-repetitious, in as much as, the circumstances would never be twice the same. i.e. A decision to marry someone calls for reliable information, credible consideration, process of elimination and ultimate decision but, even in the event of you marrying again, it would involve a different partner and many changed factors and your previous analyses therefore would not be applicable hence it would not be a POLICY.

The Final decision making category is a JUDGEMENT and this is a decision that resists all other techniques and processes and must be made, after exhausting the analyses, on intuition and gut feeling.

The situation has now reached critical stage:

> A decision has to be made

> You know how to make a decision

> The question is no longer

> > *Can You do it?*

> The question is:

> > *Do You want to do it!*

Understanding Change

There are people whose clock has stopped. If you really study them you can almost tell what time it stopped at by their dress, speech, points of reference etc. Men who still favour flared trousers or women who cling to the padded shoulders popularised in *Dynasty* because their finest moments were experienced when it was the fashion. If an older police officer catches you speeding he will still ask 'Who do you think you are, Stirling Moss?' and I actually heard a man refer to a Glasgow taxi in 1997 as a Joe Baksi. (Big Joe was an American boxer who came to London in the 1950s and walloped the hide off Bruce Woodcock.)

Musical preference is a real give away of course as are dance styles. I spent a number of years working on the U.K. cabaret circuit and, whilst I have never thought of myself as a dancer, I did keep up with trends and once actually danced on television with Lionel Blair. See I've done it again, most of you reading this don't even remember Lionel Blair as a dancer but think he's that guy who does mime games on T.V. Anyway, I recently visited a night-club and found I was totally out of touch. For one thing there was so much noise coming out of the speakers you couldn't hear the music and for another there was so much vibration coming through the floor you just stood there and it passed for dancing. The fact that I even commented on this dated me.

Frank Sinatra once electrified the dance world and increased the popularity of matrimony when he sang:

> *Love and Marriage, Love and Marriage*
> *Go together like a Horse & Carriage*

Crap patter now because this is the age of internal combustion engines and parents endeavouring to extol the virtues of marriage are often viewed simply as relics from another era when knowing 'Old Hieds' rolled in laughter at the suggestion of someone, some-day actually running a mile in four minutes.

You have to embrace change, accept progress, believe in your ability to adopt and recognise that the only thing that is constant is change. There is a great saying that goes:

> *The road to success is always under construction.*

I like that because it tells it as things really are. You must know what you want and you must know why you want it and you should have a plan as to how you will get it but you must also be prepared to accept that, in the words of the Wee Man with the Magic Pen:

The best laid plans of mice and men gang aft aglae!

There is absolutely no doubt that any intelligent human being who encounters quality information as to how they can maximise their potential will want to achieve more, but I am convinced the majority of those who fail to grasp the opportunity, default because they are incapable of changing their ways. We are creatures of habit and it is extremely difficult to change a lifelong habit.

Having studied this area and recognising my own shortfalls I have put together a formula for change:

$$C = D + V + FS + E + NS$$

C stands for **Change**

Job, Relationship, Attitude.

Whatever it is you want to change, write it down in statements with supportive facts which provide a clear understanding.

D is for **Discomfort**

I truly believe that very few of us will change if we are comfortable with what we have or where we are. Imagine sitting in the sunshine somewhere in the Mediterranean with a free bar and your mate suggesting you try somewhere else. I truly believe we only give serious consideration to change when we are uncomfortable and even then we would rather have the devil we know than the devil we don't so we need the V.

V is for **Vision**

We must create a quality mental picture of a better way or a better place before we will move from what we do or where we are. Sometimes we can make ourselves discontented and uncomfortable through longing for something better and that is an excellent technique for motivating change. You can use this to make any other person, group of people or even a whole organisation change if you are good at selling a dream.

New job, improved self esteem with unabounding confidence, an incredible relationship, positive attitude, improved income, better house, whatever your vision of improvement is, write it down in great detail with enthusiastic and optimistic terminology.

Todays' society tends to be a bit soft and change is something many find painful because they continually dwell on everything they enjoyed in their old job or in their last house or whatever. When this happens, friends and relatives tend to sympathise and so perpetuate the feeling of 'Poor Me'.

FS is for First Step

Once you have accepted your present situation as less than totally desirable and you further advance your interest in changing by creating a vision of how much better it could be, you will have established an energised focus and will be eager to do something about it. That is when you require direction and information which will permit you to take the first step towards your goal.

List every conceivable step you can think of to help you reach your visualised improvement. Possible inclusions might be to seek the advice of an older or more experienced person in some area and that could well be the FIRST STEP. Once you have completed your list, attempt to prioritise the steps by attaching numerals 1, 2, 3 etc. and then take the FIRST STEP.

E is for Effort or Energy

You now feel uncomfortable with your lot, you have a clear vision of what you would prefer and you know the first step to take towards a change for the better. You have to make the effort to take that First Step and you have to put some energy into it.

NS is for Next Step

Always remember that a marathon is just a series of single steps. You have now decided you want to change some aspect of your life and you have a clear vision of what you would like to change it to. You have taken the first step and have decided to put genuine effort into it. From here on it is only a matter of identifying the next step and taking it.

Revisit you previous list of 'steps to take' and revise it. Do this continually as your change is taking place.

Always bear in mind that change is constant.

Would an Evaluation Change Anything?

Do you understand the intended purpose of what you have read so far?

- Was the purpose achieved?
- Was the message relevant to you?
- Can you use this information?
- Will you use this information?
- How will you use this information?
- Where and when will you use it?

Dependent on how far down that list you answered positively you should now choose from:

- Progress to the next stage
- Read the previous chapters again
- Think about changing something

CHAPTER SEVEN

The Car and the Great Thinker

W E CAN CONSUME the fruit but we must nurture the plant that bears the fruit other wise – no more fruit!

Machines & Technology are the fruit of the human mind

I am fascinated by this piece of art-work showing the great thinker sitting on the bonnet of a car. It never fails to astound me that the mind of the man species could put together the concept of the internal combustion engine. Install the power unit and develop the car to the state of excellence it has reached and to a time where it is not only accepted but, in many instances, understood.

Where a high percentage of modern society not only use this invention but depend on it and maintain the basic mechanics to keep their car running, yet, these same people never ever stop to think that this phenomena is powered by a very basic mechanical version of the human internal combustion engine.

The simple process involved in internal combustion is the compression of a volatile substance until it reaches a combustible state then sparking it off with control and direction over the resulting explosion. Whether this explosion takes place in one of the cylinders of David Couthards' Formula One car and pushes the con rod attaching the piston to the fly wheel and turning the main-shaft that ultimately powers the wheels of the fastest car in the world or ignites an original idea within the thinking process of a human mind, the result is the same and it produces a surge of immediacy, supportive energy and propels the host vehicle with a powerful thrust.

The dynamic ability of a tiny spark to move a ton of metal is what we have harnessed when the car is the host vehicle but, when your internal combustion engine starts, it physically and mentally empowers you and, so long as you provide the engine with fuel and spark, it will continue to convert, first into energy and then, into dynamic action.

Although many select their car by body design and extras, it would be a fool who did not recognise that the most essential part of the vehicle is the power pack or the engine. In the case of a human being, the power pack is the thinking process and that is what creates all and everything for the person. You could have a beautiful body but you are going nowhere if you don't get the power pack sparking. Sure you can fill your life with elegant clothes and impressive accessories just as the Porche driver can add the CD players and the in-car computer but that same stylish roadster is going to feel pretty stupid if he has to be towed in by a trucker because his/her engine doesn't function.

Continuing down the lines that the great thinker might be following as he perches on the bonnet of that car. Doesn't it seem strange that the average car owner can give you a much more detailed account of the working parts, the maintenance and service record etc. of his/her vehicle than they can of their own body. We all know we have to service the car after a certain mileage or the trade will not credit the vehicle with the same value as other models of a similar age. We all know which fuel to put into our own car and we all know we have to check the oil and the tyre pressures and the brake fluid levels and so on and so on, but how many of us check out our own blood pressure and truly understand the purpose of good fuel for our body? How many of us recognise that, if we don't have servicing at certain mileage, we will not be of the same value as others who are in our age group?

It doesn't stop with the engine.

Moving is essential because standing still means you are going nowhere.

Moving fast is preferable to moving slow but only if you are moving in the desired direction

Even if you are an all action, energised thinker, it is just possible you are no more effective than a car with no steering wheel. Sometimes you will be passing everyone at a considerable rate of knots but other times you will appear to be careering down hill or heading for a brick wall and apparently clueless as to what you can do to correct it.

The answer is to have, not only a good engine but, top class steering gear and, in the case of the human vehicle:

The steering gear is your personal plan.

Knowing what you want, knowing why you want it, taking the time to research and establish that it is achievable and then laying down step by step goals to reach your desired destination.

Now you have your engine tuned and your steering equip ment in order

Let's stop going round the roundabouts and start burning rubber.

Unfair? Why? You reckon all is not equal out there on the great motorway of life because some are driving Jaguars and others are in wee Puntos'. Sure! That is true, just as some are born beautiful and others have to rely on the fading light but, and I assure you this is a fact, not every Jaguar driver drives their car flat out and the very fact that it is a prestigious and expensive, elegant and desirable possession is very often the very factor that curtails their speed and their attitude. They sport their car rather than use it to transport them to where they want to go in the shortest possible time. The Punto can be driven flat out and pass many a car with vastly superior specifications.

You might not consider yourself as beautiful, well endowed, connected or gifted as many another but, whilst they preen and postulate, you can kick ass and consummate every thing you deserve in life. A great many people I have met in life who were born with some apparent advantage have grown to depend on it and, as a result, have become less capable and less responsible with low achievement, low self esteem and an extremely stressful life because they have never fulfilled their expectancy.

Remember the car is as good as its' engine and the principal purpose of your body is to carry the head.

Now lets' check the headlights. Are you seeing things clearly?

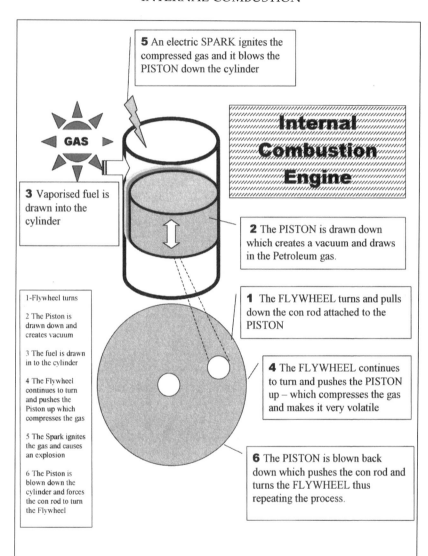

5 An electric SPARK ignites the compressed gas and it blows the PISTON down the cylinder

GAS

Internal Combustion Engine

3 Vaporised fuel is drawn into the cylinder

2 The PISTON is drawn down which creates a vacuum and draws in the Petroleum gas.

1-Flywheel turns

2 The Piston is drawn down and creates vacuum

3 The fuel is drawn in to the cylinder

4 The Flywheel continues to turn and pushes the Piston up which compresses the gas

5 The Spark ignites the gas and causes an explosion

6 The Piston is blown down the cylinder and forces the con rod to turn the Flywheel

1 The FLYWHEEL turns and pulls down the con rod attached to the PISTON

4 The FLYWHEEL continues to turn and pushes the PISTON up – which compresses the gas and makes it very volatile

6 The PISTON is blown back down which pushes the con rod and turns the FLYWHEEL thus repeating the process.

Man Invented
Mechanical Perpetual Motion

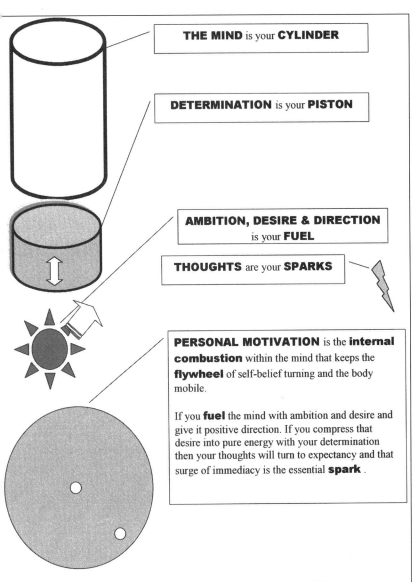

THE MIND is your **CYLINDER**

DETERMINATION is your **PISTON**

AMBITION, DESIRE & DIRECTION is your **FUEL**

THOUGHTS are your **SPARKS**

PERSONAL MOTIVATION is the **internal combustion** within the mind that keeps the **flywheel** of self-belief turning and the body mobile.

If you **fuel** the mind with ambition and desire and give it positive direction. If you compress that desire into pure energy with your determination then your thoughts will turn to expectancy and that surge of immediacy is the essential **spark** .

The Mind of a Successful Man
Is an Internal Combustion Engine

Want to try another Evaluation?

Do you understand the intended purpose of what you have read so far?

- Was the purpose achieved?
- Was the message relevant to you?
- Can you use this information?
- Will you use this information?
- How will you use this information?
- Where and when will you use it?

Dependent on how far down that list you answered positively you should now choose from:

- Progress to the next stage
- Read the previous chapter again
- Consider changing your fuel or think about creating a spark

So establish exactly what you want

- What do you want out of life?

- What do you need to help you get what you want?

- Do you need an idea? Do you have an idea but need a strategy?

- Do you just need a change of direction?

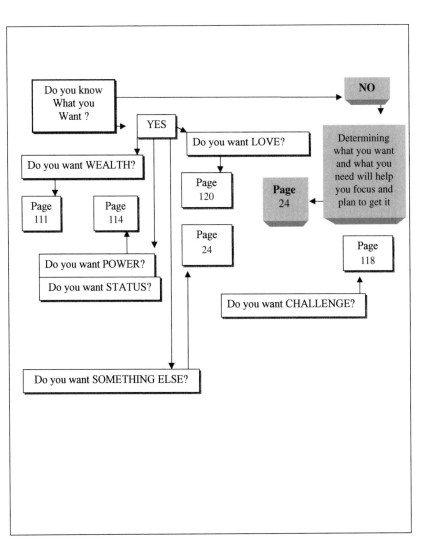

Returning to the very basics of personal achievement it is essential to understand that the majority of people do not get what they want out of life because they do not expect to get what they want but rather strive for what they need and just dream of what they would have preferred.

If you cast your mind back over any time in your life and allow your memory recall to relate the facts without your intrusion or enhancement, isn't it true that you have usually got what you expected to get. When you had a school exam approaching and you were cramming away in earnest hope of scraping a pass, isn't it true that you mentally arrivedat a decision and inwardly settled for something that seemed inevitable. And isn't it absolutely true that whatever you expected the results to be was fairly damn close to what you got?

I am convinced that, in this life, we cannot take it for granted that we will ever get what we want nor be sure we will get what we need and I sincerely hope, for most of our sake, that we never get what we deserve, but I expect to get, and I expect you to get, a fair amount of what we expect to get.

You do not get what you want in this life
You get what you expect!

My theory is that we curtail our efforts to achieve what we expect to achieve and develop a, *What's the use of trying any harder,* attitude because what we expect is what we believe in. You simply think something through, maybe a job application or a marriage proposal and you make an assessment of your own abilities, strengths and qualifications. You refer to your past achievements and shortfalls and you make a decision which determines what you expect to happen. If you expect to be unsuccessful then you go about the task in the manner of someone who expects to fail. You exude negativity.

If you think you have what it takes to get this job and you have someone in a high place speaking for you and your expectations are high, it is reasonable to assume you will take great pains to make sure you represent yourself in a very positive manner and it is reasonable to assume you will probably get the job.

The rich get richer

The rich expect to get richer. The rich think about rich things. The rich think about:

Top of the Range – Designer – Exclusive

What do the rich get? The rich get:

Top of the Range – Designer – Exclusive.

Exactly what they expect!

The poor get poorer

What do the poor people expect to get?

Bills – Hardship – CRAP.

What do the poor people get? The poor people get:

Bills they cannot pay – Hardship – CRAP (and plenty of it).

Exactly what they expect!

The technique is to take time to determine what it is that you want and to take quality time to determine why you would want it. Once you know what you want, it is essential to study the required needs for the acquisition of what you want and to accurately and honestly assess your potential. You must be able to convince yourself that what you want is reachable.

It may be that it will take time. It may be that that the journey to where you want to be will be painful. It may be at the cost of other things that you hold dear but you will not set out your plan and take the appropriate action in life to get what you want unless you are convinced that it is possible.

Once you know it is achievable then you never ever ask yourself that demoralising, self doubting question:

Can I do this?

You may ask yourself:

Do I want to do this?

That is a question of choice and if you decide not to do whatever has to be done to achieve your dream:

You will at least have removed the frustration of having been denied the opportunity.

Should you decide to go for it, in the knowledge that it is achievable, then you attack every task, every day, in every way with an expectation of a positive result and:

What you want and what you expect become one and the same thing.

And: **We usually get what we expect!**

WHAT DO YOU WANT?

Most people *think* they know what they want! Successful people **know** what they want!

If you are unsure of what you want and haven't really established a burning, passionate desire for something, a very good starting point is to list what you most definitely do not want.

The NEGATIVE to POSITIVE technique works on the basis that, if you concentrate on avoiding that which you dislike in the journey of life, it is reasonable to assume you will end up in a place which is totally to your liking.

Why don't' we start making lists?

Feeling listless? Make a list!

Make a list of PYOs. (*see glossary of terms*)

Once you have compiled this list, put them into categories such as:

    A   for everything involving personality conflict
    B   for areas making excessive physical demands
    C   for personal frustration

EXAMPLE:

Hate List	Why – because	Cat
Being told what to do by younger people	Because I think I deserve the same respect from those who are younger than me as I show my elders	A

Once you have categorised all your areas of discomfort then prepare a list of where. This discomfort happens most regularly.

What I dislike	Where dislike occurs
Personality conflict	When I try to explain my ideas to other members of the management team
Feelings of physical inadequacy	When younger members of staff insist on moving office furniture around
Frustration	

Now make a Negative to Positive list:

Negative	Positive	Therefore
I do not like having younger people telling me what to do and I have to accept this within my present employment	I do enjoy working with younger people when I pass on the benefits of my experience and see the improvement in their skills	I should get a position where I can train young people

110

No Idea of What you Want

List everything that could improve your city, town, village, street, home. Ask some of your friends and relatives to do the same.

What you will be compiling is a list of opportunities because everything on your lists will be some product or service that someone has expressed an interest in or a desire for and, as it is not available at present, the law of supply and demand says this is an opportunity.

List things you like doing and then re evaluate them to see if there is a career or business opportunity. It is much more likely that you will put enthusiastic effort into something you enjoy rather than something which merely offers a return.

List talents and skills you have and try to evaluate them as dispassionately as possible. We are all guilty of discrediting personal accomplishment and, because you have taken the time and made the effort to learn to play a musical instrument or make floral arrangements, cook or paint, it doesn't mean it is easy and can be done by anyone. It means that you can do it and that may represent an opportunity.

Wealth

By far and away the majority of people who attend development workshops start out believing that what they most want is WEALTH. Consider now whether or not wealth is your dream and then reconsider it with an open mind that embraces both the advantages and disadvantages of wealth.

Advantages of Wealth	Disadvantages of Wealth
Security	Envy
Always sure of food and a home	Rich people are seen as desirable targets for theft, their children are at risk of kidnapping and they are often victims of social jealousy, etc
Purchasing Ability'	
Can buy anything you want	Social Imbalance
Choice	Because they can afford to live in a more luxurious style, self made. Financial achievers often lose their social circle and are often friendless
Never having to settle for second best	
Quality	
To afford a 'Top of the Range' lifestyle	Fear of Loss
Investment	Once you have it you fear having to manage without it
Making your money do the work	

Do you really want to be wealthy or do you want only the Advantages of wealth?

Are you prepared to create a social gap between you and your best friends?

Alternatively, are you sure your friends could handle the financial gap, even if you were prepared to pay their way?

Do you think your family and your buddies could handle charity?

Possibly you don't really care, but more likely you haven't considered that aspect of wealth.

When the entire nation started out on the, 'If I won the lottery', game the majority of people reeled off seemingly well intentioned investments such as a good holiday, a better house, trust funds for their children and financial support for parents. A wee pub for Uncle Bobby and a hairdressing business for some favoured cousin and so on until one relative would be mentioned and, for the majority, this was the passionate moment, the awakening of a realistic visualisation of how a lottery win could change lifestyle values.

At the mention of this particular relative, the eyes would light up and venom would be injected into the verbally delivered fate of this unsuspecting victim. I have heard many an outburst from gentle and seemingly kindly people, who only an instant before had been unselfishly sharing their windfall with all of mankind, but when this one relative is mentioned it triggers the statement that discloses the hidden hatred:

And he is getting .... all!

The *he* referred to in such an instance is invariably the wealthiest member of the orators' family or social set and the hatred would actually move this person to give away all their riches to everyone else just to make this one person lose their financial high ground. Such is the latent hatred within the majority of people in our society for those who are perceived to have more money than them.

You consider this and decide it may be a problem but, if you are the wealthy one, it isn't your problem. O.K. Think of all the people you harbour ill feeling towards mainly because they have it and you don't. You probably have a mental list of people who think they can buy anything including you but, if you become wealthy, they will be the only people you can socialise with on an equal basis and be reasonably certain they're not just after your money.

What kind of wealth do you want?

Wealth can come in many shapes and forms and we are all familiar with terms like 'A Wealth of Experience', but, generally speaking, the word 'wealth' implies lots of spending stuff.

Money is the common denominator on which Western society is founded and operated, no matter what garbage the philosophers endeavour to confound you with. If you don't have money you cannot pay your bills and you get lots and lots of stress as a result.

So we are talking bucks here. No messing around with fancy double meanings. You want money but what form would it take, bearing in mind that the formula for achievement contains that all important ingredient: *is it achievable?*

Do you want a personal fortune or do you have visions of property accruing income and enhanced value throughout your life span? Both concepts of wealth have individual requirements and, although one could lead to the other, at the outset the plan would be very different.

Perhaps you have thoughts of a business empire supporting a wealthy persons' life style before amassing a personal fortune when sold, or you may have some other more original idea.

How would you acquire your wealth ?

Do you envisage the wealth coming through gradual accumulation with good judgement and investments or would you consider your wealth potential to lie with a more dynamic approach?

All of this has to be considered when you are setting down the bones of your plan and then the *when* question has to be addressed.

Will you give a specific time to the wealth acquisition or will it be a life long quest? Are you prepared to dedicate a certain number of years to a committed pattern?

Even when you have all of this thought through, you must again push your results through the *why* procedure. Why would you be prepared to concede five years of your life and risk the loss of your loved ones for a personal fortune? Well!

Only you could answer that.

Power

Perhaps wealth isn't what particularly turns you on. Sure you can relate to the advantages of it but, in your instance the real essence of success is power, or perhaps status.

If you have the power then possibly you control the wealth.

Let us consider power and/or status.

Power

Advantages of Power	Disadvantages of Power
Strength	Jealousy
Influence	Resistance
Self Expression	Challenge
Respect	Loss of Humour
	Energy Draining

Would you really like to have power or only the advantages of power?

What kind of Power do you want?

> Physical
> Intellectual
> Emotional
> Executive
> Political
> Sexual
> Other

How can you acquire Power?

Do you start by establishing a daily code of self discipline that maintains physical fitness? Perhaps you have aspiration to rise to professional or political station and will embark on an education programme. Alternatively you could join the credible organisations, seek to curry favour and depend on who you know when the break comes. If you do gain your high ground by this route, you would have to ask yourself if you are really powerful or the pawn of of a greater power.

Possibly you will study basic psychology, determine the control factors in other people, learn how to generate respect from others, or perhaps strike fear into others, or create an environment dependent on you.

Before you set your plan for the acquisition of power, ask yourself what you will do when you get it and ask yourself if you really are attracted to the consequences of applying that power.

Status

Advantages of Status	Disadvantages of Status
Personal Satisfaction	Loss of Privacy
Respect	Fear of losing Status
Privilege	
Feeling of Importance	
Acclaim	

Would you really like to have status or only the advantages of status?

What kind of Status do you want?

The Boss

The Winner

The Champion

Celebrity

Fame

Legend

How can you acquire Status?

Status is the position granted to an individual by a peer group, usually as a result of an exceptional achievement or a sustained effort. It cannot be claimed or demanded and it is difficult to plan for because the ultimate control factor lies with no one person but rather an accumulated perception.

Often a human performance merits recognition but is conducted with such expertise that it looks easy to the observer and therefore the deserved praise is denied. Even though the performance of a human being is recognised and the immediate peer group are prepared to elevate the individual to this higher plain, it is often some other part of their personality or lifestyle that cancels out their appeal to the wider public and their status really becomes notoriety.

Study, practise, publicity, dedication and corruption are all means and ways towards possible recognition and ultimate status but there are no guarantees in anything that depends on the perception and opinion of others. If you crave status you must prepare for challenge and recognise and learn the essential ingredient skills you need for success:

Attitude control

Communication ability

Planning

Self Discipline

The Power of an Evaluation

Do you understand the intended purpose of what you have read so far?

- Was the purpose achieved?
- Was the message relevant to you?
- Can you use this information?
- Have you decided what you want out of life yet?
- Do you know how to get it?
- What is the first action you will take?

Dependent on how far down that list you answered positively you should now choose from:

- Progress to the next stage
- Read the previous chapters again
- Ask someone you believe to have status to explain it to you

Challenge

Advantages of Challenge	Disadvantages of Challenge
Self Motivation	Failure leading to loss of Self Belief and Self Respect
Self Expression	
Self Esteem	Obsession

Do you want challenge in your life or do you just feel guilty being comfortable?

What kind of challenge do you want?

A challenger being someone who wants to be:

> A Winner
>
> A Champion
>
> The Best
>
> The First

How would you know if you are a challenger and, if you are not, how could you acquire the skills and ability to challenge?

The principle driving forces within the character of a challenger are self belief and determination. Persistence is often the discipline that is admired in a challenger and a great many positive results come from the challenger having this ability to hang on and never give in until they grind their opponent into disillusion and loss of self belief. This can best be seen in one to one sports situations such as Wimbledon or some of the great boxing encounters where the underdog absorbs the punishment and keeps coming back.

For many, these characteristics are natural but are not always an advantage because they are not consistent with the desired outcome and make the individual too competitive in inconsequential areas where they would have benefited by portraying support for another as opposed to strong challenge.

If challenge and competitive spirit does not come naturally then it is best initiated through a change of mindset and that is best acquired through the study of desired outcome. Back to that same set of focus points.

> *What do you want?*
>
> *Why do you want it?*

Being convinced it is achievable will raise the self belief whilst the answer to the other two questions will provide the purpose and the resolve to meet a challenge head on.

Feel Good

Advantages of Feel Good	Disadvantages of Feel Good
Having	Fear of Loss
Being	Self Recrimination
Doing	Guilt over the hardships of
Appreciating	others
Financial Freedon	Becoming Pretentious
Peace of Mind	
High Energy Level	
Positive Attitude	
High Self Esteem	

Do you really experience a desire for the feel good factor or does it just sound like something you would like?

Feel Good

What kind of Feel Good do you want ?

> Peace of Mind
>
> Health & Energy
>
> Financial Freedom
>
> Good Relationships
>
> Good Looks

How do you intend acquiring the feel good factor?

Feel Good comes from striking a balance of the three factors:

$$Having - Doing - Being$$

The advantages of having three feet on a tripod are obvious. The imbalance of one or two feet is equally evident.

Areas of endeavour

To feel good you can diet, exercise, develop a more generous perception of others and life in general. You can become more fastidious over your personal hygiene and become more aware of your personal concept.

> *Having* doesn't have to relate to material things.
>
> *Being* doesn't have to relate to power or position.
>
> *Doing* is simply the activation of your desires.

If you have self respect, do what you believe is right and, at all times you know you are being the best you are capable of being then, trust me, you will feel good!

Love

Advantages of Love	Disadvantages of Love
Bonding	Loss of Personal Identity
Support	Fear of Inadequacy
Understanding	Jealousy
Comfort	

Do you really want love or only the advantages of love?

Love – What is your potential (How loving are you)?

What kind of love do you want?

> Self Love
>
> Marital
>
> Parental
>
> Romantic
>
> Caring
>
> Free Love

Areas of endeavour:

> Understanding
>
> Commitment
>
> Emotional control

Love bonds two or more people together:

> Husband & Wife
>
> Parent & Child
>
> Friends
>
> Sexual Partners etc

Bonding is a powerful emotional support until one partner reneges and the other feels impossible inadequacies when denied the previous support.

I Challenge You to Evaluate Yourself as a Lover – Of Life

Do you understand the intended purpose of what you have read so far?

- Was the purpose achieved?
- Was the message relevant to you?
- Can you use this information?
- Do you now understand what you want out of life?
- How will you use this information?
- Where and when will you use it?

Dependent on how far down that list you answered positively you should now choose from:

- Progress to the next stage
- Read the previous chapters again
- Keep thinking about what you want and how you can get it until you believe it is achievable and you *Feel Good* about yourself.

> *The principle difference between Rape & Seduction*
> **Technique**

CHAPTER EIGHT

If It's in Your Nature

ONCE THERE WAS a scorpion with a problem. The scorpion wanted to find a mate in life and found himself the only scorpion on one bank of the river whilst all the other scorpions were on the opposite side.

Turning, instinctively to meet a young frog as it approached the river, the scorpion demonstrated *lateral thinking and negotiation skills* with a business offer the frog found impossible to refuse. The scorpion explained that it was in a position to sting the frog to death but would trade life for a safe passage on the back of the frog to the other bank of the river.

Naturally the frog feared his fate once the scorpion had achieved it's destination but accepted the insect's reassurances that there was nothing to be gained by killing the frog and, furthermore, he was developing a new liking for his new green travelling companion.

Communication skills came to the fore as both creatures fell into an easy conversation and exchanged views and theories on life as they found it and an excellent working relationship had been developed and teamwork employed when the frog took the scorpion on his back and set out against the flow of the water with the greatest of care to protect the smaller creature from the dangers of the fast flowing river.

Using all his strength and natural skills, the frog eventually navigated the torrents and emerged from the river to deliver his passenger safely to the dry bank, upon which the scorpion stung the frog and watched dispassionately as he lay dying.

'I should never have trusted you,' croaked the frog, 'You're a liar and a cheat.' The scorpion shook his head resignedly and told the frog the facts of life. 'I did nothing, wrong. I killed you because it's in my nature!'

Why are people surprised when a Rottwieler bites a child? That is what Rottweilers do. You get a Rottweiler puppy and you brag continually that once it grows up nobody will mess with you because this will blossom into eight stone of solid muscle with a head like a bear and a mouth like a shark.

'This dog will rip the arm off anybody who so much as sets foot on my property.' Then one day it bites you and you are surprised and what do you say?

'That's not fair, I bought it, I feed it, I take it out for walks, I love it and give it every consideration'. Well, maybe the Rottweiller recognises all that and, in appreciation of your efforts and love, it does what it does best – It bites you! That's what Rottweillers do!

So what do you do? What is in your nature? Have you surrounded yourself with people of like nature or are you toiling in un-natural surroundings?

So regularly I meet people who are not coping because they are doing something with their life that isn't natural for them. Used to be in that category myself and know first hand the feeling of working indoors when you are naturally an out of doors, fresh air kind of person. I absolutely detest keeping records and any form of accountancy but, fortunately, there are accountants who sit and chuckle to themselves in glee and orgasmic satisfaction as they number crunch and percentigise everything. My own immediate reaction to such creatures is 'Get a life', but I recognise now that they have, not only a life, but the life they want. Number crunching comes natural to them!

Two very essential facts emerge from the recognition of natural characteristics. One is that we should endeavour to understand our own natural characteristics and locate a way of life that permits us full license within this area. Then, and I am convinced only then, can we maximise our potential, be happy, be fulfilled and be everything we are capable of being. You will find that the majority of people who are successful are working within an area they feel is right for them although I must warn against mistaking this for comfort. There are a number of species on this planet who seek only to find comfort. They live a parasitic life on the back of other creatures who are capable hunters and providers and invariably these comfort seekers become slow, fat and lazy and easy prey for their predators. This happens because comfort is not natural.

Man, the species, has five senses, an intuitive awareness and a nervous system all built into and attached to this incredible, head-top, computer between the lugs. All of this is in our natural design to protect us to make us aware of imminent danger and to equip us with the ability to seek out and establish safe high ground with an abundance of provision. When that is achieved, the equipment turns to protection mode and security is constant vigil. This is the natural function of the human mind. This comes natural and will always take you to the highest point in your ability factor but settling for comfort is not natural, it is the product of Western society that makes us fat, lazy and vulnerable to our predators.

Peer pressure, envy, jealousy, low self esteem are just a few of the silent predators consuming so many people like a cancer whilst they become totally time consumed in their defence against the more obvious roaring lions such as personal relationships and immediate relative poverty. You have to deal with the raging lions but don't let it become an all consuming thought process because you will hear and see them coming and the outcome will be invariably determined by the initial strategy, but these other, self created, mental predators, consume you from the inside out.

That Rainbow song will have to go. It slows the whole thing down

Ed Wynn – MGM Producer of the classic movie: *Wizard of Oz*

Perception is Reality

Personal Appearance and Behaviour determine how others see you.

As Perception is Reality to most of us, how people see us and believe us to be, determines what they think of us, how they rate us and how they determine our value to them.

How others evaluate you will govern their support of your efforts.

Women who wear short skirts!

Women who wear short skirts are presumed by men to be women who wish men to look at their legs. *Right Guys? Correct Girls?*

Women who want men to look at their legs are presumed by men to be women who are mentally aware of their physical attraction and wish it to be recognised by the opposite sex. *Correct Girls? Right Guys?*

The kind of men who are interested in women who are mentally aware of their physical inclinations, clock this person and evaluate their *Personal Appearance and their Behaviour Pattern* and determine what, if any, extra value this person could bring to their life. *Right Guys? Correct Girls?*

If the sensory input through this males' eyes stimulates any kind of *Positive Visualisation*, he may decide to fulfil the lady's' desired outcome when she selected her personal marketing image. He might, for instance, choose to re-enforce her opinion of her personal appearance by applying a little male bonding patter:

'How's it going Darling! By the way has anyone ever told you that you are sitting on the end of a pair of stotting pins.'

The Female recipient, being totally unaware of the male mental process preceding this salutation and appraisal, could react in a number of ways because she will initially evaluate the male appraiser by his *Personal Appearance and Behaviour. Correct Girls ?*

If indeed the lady has worn the skirt for the exact purpose the gentleman has figured, she will see him as a positive result and a desirable and reliable source of constructive perception, accept his statement, and possibly enter into conversation. Snap! Bingo! Come Fly with Me!

If, however, the lady has perhaps been visiting her daughter, spilled something nasty on her designer, ankle length, tweed skirt and has been obliged to borrow something from her trendy daughter, which she now feels self conscious wearing – she is very likely to perceive this intruder into her privacy as a sarcastic moron. *Correct Girls* ?

There is more than a fair chance he will receive the kind of response that might make him doubt his abilities in the field of personality and psychological prognosis. *Correct Girls?*

There are unlimited permutations to the confusion between any two people as they assess each other, and this particular female may even be from another part of the world and see him as a quaint speaker of some forgotten tongue. For that matter, she may fully understand him and burst out laughing because he appears as some kind of nutter. Alternatively, she may not fully understand the vernacular and mistake the urgency of his approach as a warning that two bouncing sharp ended objects might just suddenly protrude from the surface area of her seat and puncture her beautiful bum.

Perception is truth – You must think about how you want to be seen and how you want to be thought of and dress and behave in that fashion.

Even more so if you are uneasy or apprehensive about the company you are in. People who have never met you before can only base their assessment of you on their sensory input.

What they see and what they hear you saying and how you react in situations will be, to them, the real you. Always start to plan your *Personal Appearance* by establishing the *Desired Outcome*.

How do others have to see you to be sufficiently impressed that you are the correct person to fill whatever role they control and you desire? If you wish to find a :–

Partner

Financial Backer

Customer

Friend

How would you have to appear? Would you want to look and behave as though you were:

Knowledgeable

Enthusiastic

Happy

Highly Motivated

Young

Mature

Experienced

Sympathetic

These lists could go on forever and they raise chain reaction questions for the individual because you may not wish to appear the same to all people. You may for instance want to appear mature and stable in your employers eyes but young, happy go lucky, carefree and one incredibly adventurous and exciting, devil may care, bundle of fun in your social life.

I happen to be particularly proud of one young protégé of mine who now works in management within a very large organisation. In his early thirties, this guy is totally committed to his work. It is the mainspring of his lifestyle and he takes immense pleasure from his ability to conceive a project and see it through to the end. He was devastated when his enthusiasm was interpreted by his upliner, from the dinosaur era, as devious because his reluctance to take a vacation indicated that he feared audit in his absence whilst, in reality, there was no holiday he could possibly have dreamed of that would have charged his batteries to the extent that completion of his project would.

When I was young I sported long hair and a beard and was denied several good jobs because I refused to modify either. Like my folk singing contemporaries, I required the fuzz on the face and the smelly Arran knit jumper to establish acceptance and, as a result, was probably categorised by the SBS and the LEP (*see* glossary) as a rebellious flea farmer.

The SBS and the LEP are a kind of secret society with incredible power but no recognised organisation. If you decide to stand against them it is unlikely you will ever have a special stamp issued in commemoration of your efforts. I have often tried to crack their code but am convinced it is no easier than cracking a smile on their face.

I have, through the years, modified the beard, and nature now denies me a wide range of coiffure but, in reviewing my life, I would have to accept that the beard has played a significant part in shaping my career, my relationships with others and my life in general.

It is not always immediately apparent to an individual but, with the benefit of hindsight, I could have achieved my goals much easier, and certainly much sooner, had I considered what my goals were and how others would have to perceive me if they were to find me exciting, appealing or even acceptable.

What do you see?

Two people running! Great! Is he chasing her with criminal intent or with some other devious purpose in mind? Is he pursuing her because she has stolen something? Are they both running towards something they desire or away from something they fear? Do the expressions on their face tell you anything? There is a clue in their dress perhaps or are you basing your perception on some personal experience or do you find the sight of older people running humorous or do you really not give a threepenny whotsit for what they are doing?

Do you see any value in an Evaluation?

Do you understand the intended purpose of what you have read so far?

- Was the purpose achieved?
- Was the message relevant to you?
- Can you use this information?
- Will you use this information?
- How will you use this information?
- Where and when will you use it?

Dependent on how far down that list you answered positively you should now choose from:

- Progress to the next stage
- Read the previous chapter again
- Self Destruct

Remember the toes you stand on today
May be attached to the legs
That supports the arse
You have to kiss – Tomorrow!

Women

Women are incredible motivators!

I make this statement from a personal point of view because, throughout my life, I have done more to please a woman, to attract a woman, to extract a compliment from a woman or to shut a woman up than I have ever been prepared to do for either another man or myself.

Having made this statement it is my honest belief that the majority of people, if they answered honestly, would have to say that a great deal of what they have achieved was done to please or allay pressure put on them by another person. There is a very true saying in the world of personal development that all our real problems speak back to us. In other words they are other people.

I believe men are supposed to be motivated by women.

I think this is a healthy and natural state of affairs and I have never questioned it. I have not always accepted that women were motivated by men however and truly believe that the female is much more inclined to dress and perform socially to impress, to compete with or to be accepted by other women and, furthermore, I would say that women very often do all of these things to create 'personal feel good' whereas men dress and perform socially to support an image.

I expect the majority of us would agree we have been motivated at some point in our life by our mothers and I can look back on times when my mother assured me that if I ate all my crusts I would have curly hair. She lied of course and that would have been unforgivable had it not achieved the desired result of enhancing my dietary habits. My mother also raised me to recognise the Golden Rule. 'Always', she used to say, 'Always, when in doubt or strange company, apply the Golden Rule'.

I grew up believing that everyone knew the Golden Rule but it would appear that there are a few versions around such as, 'He who has the gold makes the rules'. But our version is the universal, 'Do unto others as you would have them do unto you'. It seems pretty good advice until you practice it and it suddenly means something very different.

It means that if you treat everybody as you like to be treated you are not giving a toss about how they would like to be treated. Consider that well before you voice an objection.

You are holding a house warming party and have invited all your new neighbours, your bank manager who helped get the mortgage, your three best business clients, your boss and the one relative you have who might leave you money.

Now you value your driving license very highly because it is a necessity to maintain your income and, furthermore, you have just moved into a rather remote spot where there is no public transport.

You absolutely detest being embarrassed into drinking alcohol unless you are in your own home and you have always appreciated events where alcohol was kept to the minimum and never pushed at the guests. That is how you like to be treated at a party so, applying Mum's Golden Rule, you prepare a dandelion and guava punch with bananas for dipping and you play Blue Peter's Early Learner's Recorder Tutor as backing music because that is currently one of your passions.

Not being a particularly great communicator you have always enjoyed an evening where there was some organised participation so you suggest everybody dips their banana, with a prize for those who spear a guava, and get everyone playing *I Spy* and *Mrs McGrunty's Cat*.

Of course you could keep nipping away for a wee guddle of the good stuff yourself because you are at home and getting totally blitzed out of your skull in your own house is something you are quite partial to.

At this party, by doing unto others as you would that they would do unto you, they would probably feel like doing unto you something you never planned for the bananas but might help with the high notes on the recorder.

The Platinum Rule, which places higher in the pecking order than the Golden Rule, would be: 'Do unto others as they would like to be done unto' and there is a fair chance they might just do unto you as you would like to be done unto.

Consider how often you have applied the Golden Rule in life and lost out when you might have achieved a positive result had you applied the Platinum Rule?

Make a list and then make a decision which rule you will apply in the future.

My Mother loved to talk, and she would have peeled beans for some social chatter. She considered herself to be therapeutically excellent in this area. My mother would talk to anyone, anywhere, about anything – whether they wanted to or not. If anyone visited our home they would find themselves in the kitchen with a cup of tea and my mother would be practising what she referred to as 'Drawing them out'.

When the visitor left, she would inform us, with genuine sincerity, that they would be the better for getting all that stuff they had been bottling up out in the open. She would then proceed to give us her version of what she had just promised was in confidence. You may think this was terrible, an absolute betrayal, but my mother liked everyone she met to talk to her about their wee problems because she was interested and would show concern and therefor assumed they would be equally interested in her little challenges. She was practising the Golden Rule.

There have been many female motivators in my life and I have recently had the good fortune to work with several of them. Helen Sharman was driving home from her job as a chemist when she heard on the radio that the Russians were to consider taking a Brit on their next space mission. Helen made the phone call as soon as she reached home and started a long process whereby she had to learn to speak Russian, then train in Russia in all the high tech. applications she required before starting two years of physical conditioning and then competing with other candidates before finally being chosen as the very first female astronaut.

Rebecca Stephens was not the first woman to climb Everest but she did climb it and then went on to climb the highest mountain in every continent. When I had the good fortune to share the speakers' platform with her in Ireland I was deeply impressed, not only by her adventures, but by her *intense ability to be interested in my story.*

Muriel Bryant is one of my all time heroes because she not only achieved her goal but she achieved it against terrible odds. Starting out as an orphan in England, she married an American and had some fortune building adventures with her husband that would read like a Cecil B De Mille Adventure of the Century. Twenty years ago Muriel became the Chief Executive of ITC. (International Training in Communication) and masterminded them into financial security, new headquarters in California and status and membership in virtually every country in the world. Muriel still travels extensively in her ITC role and when I last spoke to her she had just returned from China where she had headed a deputation. She then had a world conference planned for Minnesota before flying off to Japan where she will mastermind their first ever world conference in Communication Training. I am extremely proud to have Muriel as a friend.

For twenty-eight years I was married to Doreen and together we had many an adventure, including three sons. We were folk singing stage partners in an act that took us travelling throughout the world and, amongst many of the attributes I have her to thank for, is the courage to fight against the odds. She taught me how to swim when I was petrified of even standing under a shower.

I meet many different women in my everyday activities and I openly confess I am having a wonderful love affair with every one of them. I was born a male and I rejoice in female company and I am grateful for every single one who has ever crossed my path. Even the bad tempered bitches with faces like nippy sweeties because they have helped me to appreciate the good natured ones.

At a point in my life where my personal belief was sorely challenged and my philosophy appeared to be flawed I was touched by magic and embraced by Universal Law.

A lady known as Helen appeared in my life and told me what I so desperately needed to know. She cuddled me, she nurtured me and she gave me love when it seemed there was a love famine covering the planet.

We married and entered into a wonderful world of understanding, closeness, support, love and Cullen Skink. Helen smoked as many as forty cigarettes a day for almost fifty years and I feared her health might not withstand it. She demonstrated incredible resolve and determination as she gradually cut back and finally quit the habit to again demonstrate the magnificence of human resolve. Now she spends her cigarette money on nuts for wild birds and carrots for two old horses.

All women are great. Some are greater than others and occasionally one ranks as the greatest. Anyone who makes Cullen Skink as well as Helen and as often as Helen is right up at the top in my book. If I am entitled to MP after my name then she is the PM. (*see glossary*)

Women always have to be twice as good as men to
Be given the same credit!
Fortunately this isn't too difficult !

New You – The Personal Upgrade Shop

Your Personal Development Plan

The development of a Persona Plan is possibly the most important and exciting exercise you will ever undertake.

Recognise that personal planning is why some people have so much more than others.

A 'PDP' is your opportunity to really learn about yourself and get to know, not only what you are, but also what you are capable of and, almost magically, visualise your own future.

This is the opportunity to plan and project your own future and learn how to control it.

A personal development plan is like going into a People Shop and rebuilding yourself. You can decide how you want to look, how you want to talk, where you want to live, how much money you want to earn, who you want to marry etc. etc.

Goal Setting

Tell yourself what you want. What you really, really want! If you don't know what you're aiming at, how can you hit the target?

This is at the very heart of enthusiasm. If you can identify what you most want from a:

Project,

Class,

Course,

Group,

Day,

Month,

Year

Life in general,

Planning for it will excite you and, at times of challenge, visualising the realisation of your goal will inspire and motivate you.

Visualisation

I read somewhere that Ronald Reagan attended the opening of the Epcot Centre in Disneyland and made some statement of regret that Walt Disney had never seen this incredible development, to which the brother of the legendary cartoonist replied. 'Walt did see it.'

Every single man made achievement on this planet started with a thought and progressed through one persons' ability to see the outcome, to visualise the finished project. It is this clear visualisation, this foresight, this visionary skill that excites the human brain and motivates an individual.

It is this individuals' ability to communicate their vision to others who possess the technical skills which effectively motivates a team, an organisation or even a nation.

Such is the immense and awesome power of the mind of a single human being to effectively change the world that it therefor must follow that the same mental process can effectively control positive change in the outcome of the individual.

The principle function of the human body is to carry the head!

Get it right in your mind and the body will support it. If you have your basics clear, understand what you want and why you want it and you have done all that was necessary to understand the viability of your goals, visualisation is now an essential step in your progress. Seeing clearly where you are going and all you will gain by going there. Seeing clearly all the benefits, experiencing the pleasure and embracing the enhancement will motivate you and inspire you when the going is tough. Visualising the benefits of the outcome will energise you when you are tiring and focus your direction when you are lost.

How do you Visualise?

In the workshops and seminars I conduct all over the world it never fails to amaze me that so many people believe they cannot visualise and I repeatedly have to demonstrate that we all visualise, on a regular basis every day, in very ordinary sets of circumstances.

You take the preparation of a meal for an example. You have friends coming for dinner and you want to make the occasion a bit special. You run through a menu in, what might be referred to as, your minds' eye. – You are visualising the reaction to your food.

When the ladies go shopping for a new outfit for that special occasion you might find them in their favourite boutique standing in front of a full length mirror, holding a series of dresses in front of them. They are visualising how they will look on the night.

Driving through unfamiliar territory and you are forced to ask a total stranger for directions. They throw their eyes up and think for a moment and then they start to guide you, something along the lines of, third left, second right and straight through the first set of traffic lights and, just when you get your head round that lot, they change it to first right, third on the left and then right at the lights. You see – They are visualisng the route.

People visualise all the time but only a small percentage have control over their visualisations and, because they consistently use visualisation, they become better and better at it and learn to add detail.

Once you are fluent and familiar with the control of your dreams and capable of designing them, understanding, adjusting and truly experiencing them, your next step is to transpose the mental image onto paper and set down a plot or a road map which you have visualised as the necessary route to your desired outcome.

It is reasonable to assume that if you visualise yourself running twenty five miles in two hours that you would have to be capable of visualising yourself running twelve miles in an hour and, if you can visualise yourself running twelve miles in one hour, you would have to be capable of mentally believing yourself capable of a mile every five minutes and, through this process, you gradually break your big goal down to more immediate targets which can be worked on.

Take four people with four very different desired outcomes. Each capable of visualising what they want and through this visualisation, capable of experiencing it as though it had already become reality. Our four participants know now what they want more than anything in the world and they have agonised over why they have such desires and have justified them to themselves. Each if them could now be described as passionate about what they intend achieving.

Anne wants to climb Everest, not because she is a mountaineer, but because, as a twenty year old journalist, she will gain the kind of acclaim as a specialist writer that would bring sufficient financial rewards and acceptance within her chosen field to support a lifestyle she otherwise could not afford.

John owns, operates and drives a retail fish van and works round the clock. He is twenty seven now and his ambition is to be financially independent and retire by the age of forty five, when he reckons he will still be young and fit enough and able to afford to do whatever he wants, wherever he wants and enjoy a fuller life than his present environment could ever support.

Helen wants to create a pottery in the remote countryside with living accommodation and training facilities for young people to learn the enjoyment of living off the land and creating something original with their hands. She feels these standards are missing from society and would very much like to see her idea adopted on a national basis. She realises that her main station is the acquisition of a suitable site, the funding and the support of her first base and, at fifty two, she fully recognises the time element but believes her dream is possible because she has been in such a place many times through her visualisation.

Bill wants to build his own house. He has dabbled in DIY and restored two houses to a state that they sold on at increased value. Now he would like to design, plan and build his own house, with his own hands. Partly because he sees it as in investment but mainly because he knows he would feel immense pride and great satisfaction to be living in a house which he had totally constructed on a piece of ground where previously there was nothing.

Each will now have to apply a time limit for there achievement otherwise it is no more than a fanciful dream. Something we are all good at recounting. Something we talk about with enthusiasm and warmth and swear we will do it – Some day?

CASE STUDY

Anne	
Long Term Goal	**To climb Everest**
When?	*Within six years*
Mid Term Goal	*To be part of a major mountaineering expedition*
When?	*Within Three Years*
Short Term Goal	*Acquire Maximum Physical Fitness*
When?	*Within a year*
Immediate Goal	*Join club and collect information*

The inspirational part of this plan is Annes' ability to visualise, not only the achievement of conquering Everest, but the enhanced lifestyle as a result and an aftermath of the event.

It is this visionary quality that must be developed to keep her ener-gised and focussed through the painful and boring part of her plan.

Her intermediate goals would be progress targets along the way between the time spaced goals and would act like milestones i.e. Between her Short and Mid term goals she would have intermediate goals to scale mountains that would toughen her up and draw attention to her ability.

John

Long Term Goal	**Retire with Financial Independence**
When?	*Age 45*
Mid Term Goal	*Build business to million per year turnover*
When?	*Age 36*
Short Term Goal	*Acquire Business Funding*
When?	*Age 30*
Immediate Goal	*Maximise immediate potential*

John has laid his plan with a very clever, built in, capacity to monitor progress. He has laid his targets in parallel to his age and therefore has an automatic progress chart. If we could see his intermediate goals they would probably include buying out the opposition and adding additional services such as home delivery with an ultimate plan to make the business an attractive buy-out prospect.

Helen

Long Term Goal	**Training Craft Centre**
When?	*Within eight years*
Mid Term Goal	*Gain funding credibility*
When?	*Within Two Years*
Short Term Goal	*Gain experience and contacts*
When?	*Within a year*
Immediate Goal	*Disengage from all previous commitments*

Due to her age, Helen cannot afford to set her ultimate date too far ahead. She has no previous experience and is starting from scratch but the effective part of her planning is in her immediate action.

Bill

Long Term Goal	**Build his own house**
When?	*Within two years*
Mid Term Goal	*Purchased the site & secured the finance*
When?	*Within six months*
Short Term Goal	*Complete the plans/ drawings*
When?	*Within three months*
Immediate Goal	*Completely clear all outstanding projects*

Bill has a very imminent goal and is probably basing much of his finance on the assumption that he can complete the work within the allotted time. There will be planning permissions and various official areas to contend with and this type of goal setting must contain alternative routes should any challenge become too threatening. The intermediate goals will be continually changed and there could be a great deal of stress involved because of the time restriction but the inspirational element is that the goal does not end with the completion of the house but rather begins so that, although the building is depicted as the long term goal, it is, in reality, the immediate goal of a much larger and longer term vision.

Intermediate Goals are many, varied and essential as supports and bridges between the other areas of progress.

Immediate Goals are the things you plan to do to:

Get the show on the road!

Once you decide on your most desired outcome you have to visualise these goals and add details and more details until the reality of your dreams become something you are totally familiar with, something you know exists, is possible and believable then, and only then, you will have the same mindset as successful people.

Your desire to touch and hold what has become so special and precious to you, will drive you, motivate and energise you, to do all that is necessary to reach that special category.

It is sensationally simplistic but the power of simplicity is awesome.

You just have to want to be successful enough. You have to set goals within goals.

Immediate goals might be as basic as making enquiries and glean ing information,

Short term goals see you taking the first action.

Mid term goals encourage you to intensify your efforts,

Intermediate goals prevent disillusionment and provide stimulus for the final push to whatever you have set your heart on.

Quality goal setting takes time because you have to dig deep within yourself and question your desires to make certain that what you have set out for yourself really appeals and isn't some mental panacea or a scenario that impresses your partner or your parents or your employer – not even your lover.

It has to be what the real, deep down you want out of life. It has to be something you become passionate about.

GIVE IT ALL YOU'VE GOT!

FAILING TO PLAN IS PLANNING TO FAIL.

Always start with what you know best!

If you can't beat them – arrange to have them beaten!

It may be that there is some part of your plan which seems unsurmountable to you. Don't panic. No one person can do everything. Who do you know who knows something you need to know?

This is called NETWORKING

We all, at times, are intimidated by ambitious goals. You can never see yourself achieving something that seems so far off. This can usually be overcome by focusing on a singular outcome and breaking the goals down into smaller, more achievable, increments.

A typical example of incremental movement towards ultimate success is the marathon. Started by the first step and consisting, not of twenty six miles, but rather a multiple of single steps.

The most important step is the first one because that constitutes a commitment. The last step is the achievement..

A   Think about it, break it down into stages and make a plan.

B   Start immediately. This constitutes a commitment.

C   Make a list of your weaknesses and then link them to people or organisations you know who can help.

D   Consider what you can negotiate with. What strengths do you have to offer in return for help or support?

First Get to Know What You Are – Right Now!

Personal Development Plan

The Road Map, Instruction Book and Guide from where you are right now to where you want to be!

Personal Assessment is the starting point: The purpose of this assessment is to instigate an honest perception of yourself and not to 'smart-answer' or endeavour to impress any other person.

Personal Goal Analyses

Time to look at your own goals. Consider the following questions:

What are my uppermost goals ?

Where and with whom do I spend most of my time ?

What do we talk about most ?

Are my words and actions consistent with my goals ?

What is my family/social group's major purpose

What is the big current challenge in my life ?

What attitudes, habits, beliefs, comfort zones, self talk and goals need to be adjusted to overcome this challenge?

Once you have quality goals, decisions become easy to make because you know where you are going and you know how to get there and the decision is focussed on this outcome.

Will it take me closer to my goal

Yes or No

Nothing else matters.

Your goals are the essence of your existence

Your reason for being

Your major definite purpose in life.

Yes it will take me closer to my goal

Yes I will do it !

Talking to the Mirror

Personal Development is making an impressive, attitude changing, impact on your life by giving serious consideration to the basic disciplines which contribute to the effective performance of a successful person.

The first essential step is to produce a credible overview of your present life skills and associated abilities and create both an understanding of what exactly requires upgrading and a means of demonstrating progress at a later stage.

The initial assessment is your personal perception of your ability within a range of disciplines. As each of these disciplines are defined, you should grade yourself in accordance to your own ability. Being absolute mastery within a discipline and indicating no skill whatsoever, each must be scored with at least one point and no more than eight.

The wheel is an extremely effective way of seeing clearly what shape your life is in and can be effectively used by taking eight elements from any given area. In this instance you will consider the hub as zero and the parameter as eight.

Place a cross on each spoke according to your score for that discipline. Then join the crosses to make as close to a wheel as possible.

Once you have formed the shape consider it as you would the wheels of your car or a bicycle and ask yourself if the vehicle would run smooth with such wheels.

1. COMMUNICATIONS includes listening skills and the ability to hold another persons' interest and impart information

2. INTEGRITY is setting values and living to these standards.

3. DECISION MAKING starts when you open your eyes in the morning and decide what to wear and what to eat for breakfast. It continues all day until you decide to go to bed. Can you make a decision or do you procrastinate?

4. FOCUS is the ability to remain constant, to resist distraction and to have definite direction.

5. PROBLEM SOLVING involves both lateral and analytical thinking Can you be detached, impartial and open minded?

6. SELF DISCIPLINE – taking personal responsibility for your actions.

7. TIME MANAGEMENT – Making the most of available time. Prioritising.Planning your time and sticking to your plan.

8. VIISUALISATION – Not only imagining the outcome but experiencing it

THE WHEEL

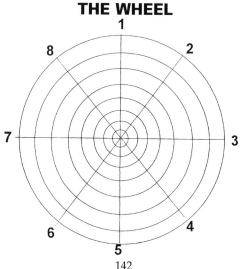

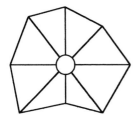

This is an irregular shaped wheel

Because this wheel is misshapen it will be a very bumpy and uncomfortable journey and, because it is small, progress will be slow.

Lifestyle: The characteristics of some-one who accepts their lot, who doesn't care, expects life to be unpleasant, and has made their mind up they are unlikely to go anywhere fast.

This is a perfectly round wheel

Because the wheel is perfectly round It will run smoothly but cover very little ground

Lifestyle: The characteristics of a person settling for an easy life with no discomfort and no real ambition

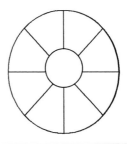

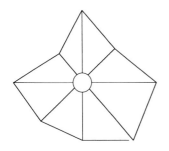

This is a large uneven wheel

This wheel would cover ground fast but do a great deal of damage on the way as well as being dangerous to those who use it and those who get in the way.

Lifestyle: The characteristics of some-one who goes for the throat and has lit-tle regard for finer feelings. This per-son could just make it but very few would stay by his side for the journey and he is odds on to crash before he gets to where he wants to go.

This is a Perfect Wheel

Because this wheel is perfectly round it will run very smoothly and because it is a large wheel it will cover a great deal of ground.

Lifestyle: The characteristics of someone who has a well balanced life and intends reaching their goal as soon as possible.

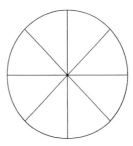

People You Meet

Because of how I live my life, I have the opportunity of meeting a great many people. All of them are exceptional because they have lived a completely original life but most of them do not consider themselves to be particularly interesting to others and , as a result, they withhold their real story and rather communicate on generally accepted subjects which they feel confident will be of interest to others and make them socially acceptable.

The result of this is the creation of ordinary people, of safe conversation, of boring and meaningless exchanges and the development of grey, sad individuals who relate everything in terms of how much they had to drink, what others were wearing or their sexual prowess.

They do not seem to realise that there are no extraordinary people born into life but some very ordinary people do things and are capable of viewing things and relating them to others in an extra special way and they become recognised as extraordinary people. All you have to do to become extraordinary is tell your story, your real story, your actual feelings, your innermost thoughts, your dreams and be prepared to take responsibility for them. Then you become not only extraordinary but very interesting, very different and very special.

I meet a great many special people and consider myself to be very privileged to have many of them as friends but it sometimes bewilders me when they find it difficult to accept that they are as special as others I may be referring to.

In company one day I had referred to conversations I had with David Coulthard, formula one driver, Graham Brown, professional strongman, John Shearer, magician and John McLaughlin, who is, amongst other things, an inventor and a wood carver. One of my colleagues interrupted to make reference to the fact that I didn't seem to know any ordinary people and explained that most of his friends knew people like accountants or consultants or lawyers. Two points were illustrated by that comment. First he was assuming that the extraordinary quality attached to these people was in how they earned their living as opposed to the fact that they were each exceptional individuals because of their attitude to life and their ability to take personal responsibility and secondly, he had not realised that he was every bit as exceptional as they were. In some respects he is more exceptional because he earns his living under the pressures of conventional political pressure and yet retains absolute positive attitude, abounding energy and tireless interest in the welfare of others without the pzazz or the glamour of a 'different' pursuit.

Many life times ago I was presenting a very homespun, folkie series on Grampian TV and suddenly was presented with a guest artiste from the glitter world of mainstream viewing. At that time, Lionel Blair was the most televised person in the U.K. and never seemed to be off the box with prestigious series from the London Palladium etc. The guy had just done a double act with Sammy Davis Junior on the Royal Command Performance, he was one of the top dancers in the entire world and I, with my grotty polo neck, beer swilling image was supposed to do something with Lionel. Straight off I put the cards on the table – No way was I dancing – Why? – Because I cannot dance. I have two left feet. I have no sense of rhythm. Besides, I had a macho image of 'Here's tae us whae's like us' – 'A man's a man for aw that and aw that' and Lionel was English and liked to camp it up.

From he arrived in Aberdeen we were friends. He is one of the most professional people I have ever met in my life and, although I doubt he realises it, he was a great influence on all of my thinking ever since. He insisted we dance together and when I repeated my protestations he asked me if I could place my right foot in front of the left and did I recognise the difference when I put the left before the right. Naturally I had to reply in the positive as I was obliged to do when he asked me if I was capable of turning right or left and recognising one from the other. We then came to an agreement that I knew my toe from my heel and could lift my feet off the ground, at least one at a time and he then pointed out that I was well capable of every single dance step and it was only a matter of sequence, timing and practise and – know what? – I danced a duet on television with Lionel Blair.

I now use this method to explain to others that, if they break anything down into manageable increments, virtually anything is possible for anyone. Take someone who proclaims their incapacity to play a musical instrument and present them with the evidence of a keyboard. Press a key and produce a note and ask them if they are capable of doing this. It seems so simple that the only difficulty is convincing them you are not TTP. Run over the a series of notes on the keyboard and ask them which note they feel they cannot play – Once they get the message that they can play every single note in every single piece of music that has ever been composed you only have to open their realisation to the fact that it is simply a matter of putting these single notes into sequence, practising their timing and, although they may never be the maestro, they can play music.

Everything in life is like that. Break it down into manageable pieces and you can do anything and I have Lionel Blair to thank for that lesson.

Perhaps the best known Scottish motivator of all time is Ally McLeod who, as Scottish Football team manager, gave the entire nation belief in itself and created an energy in the Scots that I doubt has ever been equalled in the annals of our recorded history. Ally told us we could beat the world and Ally was so good at telling us that we believed him, we believed in the team and we believed in our right to be the best. The problem as I recall it was that Ally didn't tell us how to do it and, as is always the case, the downside to great expectation is that there is further to fall and the injury of disappointment is very much greater.

When the Scottish team failed in Argentina, the Scots felt a kind of pain that only can be experienced in the mind of a person faced with failure in something that was unquestionable. The entire blame was heaped on to the man who had given them hope and poor old Ally was vilified when, in my opinion, he should have been canonised because he had created the national mindset which should have led to positive corrective attitude instead of blaming someone for their own inadequacy.

Just as in Argentine, the Scottish football squad are genuinely doing their best but the likliehood of success is very limited because what is essentially required is a total change of attitude to school and youth policy and today we are still doing the same as we did back then and, 'Do what you always did and you get what you always got.'

The lesson I learned from the Ally McLeod experience is that it is essentially important to provide a step by step plan as well as self belief otherwise energising self belief in an individual or a team is equivalent to claiming descendency from Adolf Hitler.

Having put forward a strong case for Ally, I would now like to put my hands up in the air and confess to having been the first to miscall his parentage. As a novice rider at White City speedway, I unfortunately broke my collar bone and was referred to the Victoria Hospital for physio therapy where I met a young footballer who had also broken his collar bone playing for the ill fated Third Lanark. One of the exercise techniques employed to encourage us to raise the arm above shoulder height was to strap the wrist of the offending arm, pass the strap over a high pulley and attach it to the wrist of a fellow sufferer. The idea was to gradually shorten the strap and the two participants were obliged to pull down on their side and thus raise the arm of the other, only to be rewarded by the painful reaction of your colleague who would instantly pull back to ease the considerable pain caused by raising the arm. This of course had the effect of raising the opposite participants arm and so on each caused great discomfort and pain for the other with the accompanying verbal abuse. So I can say that, at the age of fifteen, I was the first to abuse the future motivator of Scottish hopes.

Chapter Nine

Introduction to Personal Planning

THIS IS AN INTRODUCTION to yourself. A first step into Planned Personal Development It should answer many questions and provide the fundamental ability to resist the onslaught of social negatives and the self limiting beliefs that destroy most attempts to change our mindset. In short, this is about recognising who and what you really are and all you are capable of doing. This is about filing your claim for your inherited right to be the very best that you are capable of becoming.

This is about recognising your potential as an original, first edition, individual human being and realising that you are well capable of maximising that potential. This is about facing the reality of life's situation and defeating the doubts of whether you are good enough to make it all the way to your dream.

The question you will have to answer at the end of this session is not 'Can I do it?' The answer to that question and many others should have been provided in this book. The only question you have to answer for yourself is 'Do I want to do it!'

The Why – because thingamy?

BECAUSE – Every time you think a WHY it is a negative declaration and an admission that you are unsure of something. Every time you think a BECAUSE you determine your attitude and embellish positive intention.

> WHY are you doing whatever you do in life?
>
> WHY are some people, less capable than you, apparently doing much better?
>
> WHY do you always have to be the understanding one?

My idea is to reintroduce each individual, within any size of a group, team or family, to themselves, in a positive light and kindle the recognition that they are not only interesting but, within themselves, they will find the most interesting person they are ever likely to meet. This involves:

Self Assessment — Much more effective than any computer based profiling because it contains no Fear Factor.

The power and implied potential of the computer has defeated its' own purpose with psychometric profiling. Most of the American based systems require the participant to select one of a given option list of answers to a series of probing personal questions.

It is transparently obvious that the intended outcome is to generate some evaluation of the participant who, unless they happen to have nail holes in their hands and feet, will wish to convey their most preferred characteristics as opposed to their true mindset, which might include a jaundiced perception of their Chief Executives' parentage.

In short, any bubble brain will smart answer a psychometric test to produce their most desired reading and this has resulted in the programmers endeavouring to outwit this reaction by devious subplotting and has, in turn, developed counter strategies from switched on participants demanding counter-counter measures from the now demented minds of the programmers.

This circus has culminated in profiles based on preferred selection from prepared answers to questions which are so convoluted that it appears job starts, promotions and professional progress is dependent on how you think you would like your breakfast eggs prepared when Pluto is in opposition to Saturn and you are in mourning over the loss of the family budgie.

The inability to determine essential facts about an individual and their attitude through this system has escalated into the production of what is known as 180 degree or 360 degree profiles, which, in reality means they want you to ask your family members, your friends or your work colleagues what they think of you. Pretty scientific stuff ! But it is widely used because it is supplied in impressive packaging, costs a lot and therefore, by 'executhereo' must be good.

Me personally. I am never ever going to give any computer information that it might regurgitate at some future date and humiliate me, embarrass me or hang me !

The information in a Self Assessment is for the participants' eyes only, as are calculations and ultimate conclusions formed by the reader of this book.

Personal development, corporate development, team development or any other kind of development of one or a group of people has to be structured and the first step in this plan is the recognition of what the person or group are made of and where the person or team are right now. If you don't' know where you are you may know where you want to go but it is unlikely you are ever going to get there.

Life, like all modes of travel, requires either an engine or an understanding of nature. Otherwise you end up at the mercy of the elements If you have been blown about a bit and feel all washed up and a bit like a beached whale you have the two options. Come to terms with your lot and make the best of it, much as the yachtsman deals with a storm, or kick start your engine and get the hell out of it with some idea of where you're going, plenty fuel and quality steering gear to make sure you get there.

Now you should have recognised that the basis of all personal development, achievement, motivation or just plain 'getting what you want' is a plan or a carefully plotted course with an understanding of where to begin and where you want to go.

Failing to plan is planning to fail!

To rely on luck or somebody else giving it to you is to greatly reduce the chances of achievement and to totally concede control of your own destiny. The majority of people you know have never really planned what they want to do with their life and, as a result, are making the best of what they have, where they are and who they are doing it with because of how they handled what life threw at them. Most of them will justify their existence through comparison to their own peer group or other members of their family and, as long as they are no better or worse than anybody else, they will accept their lot. Probably they moan about the taxes or the next door neighbours and probably they upgrade their car occasionally and voice opinions on current events but, in the main, they settle for 'No worse than anybody else'.

How many of your acquaintances are doing what they dreamed of doing when they were infants?

How many of your acquaintances are truly living their dream?

Are you living your dream?

Is, whatever you are doing with your life, what you always wanted to do when you were a child?

Are you prepared to settle for no better or worse than anybody else.

Do you measure your potential against the standards of others?

150

Do you have belief in your own abilities?

Do you have a dream?

If you were going for a business start up you would make a plan, do some market research, set some targets and acquire the skills and support you would require. All of this comes under the heading of a BUSINESS PLAN and no self respecting financial expert would take your business seriously if you didn't have one that clearly stated who you are, what your expertise is, what experience and qualifications you have etc. etc.

If you want to live your dream you need a LIFEPLAN – A VERY PERSONAL PLAN that starts with where you are right now and how you got there. The purpose of a PERSONAL LIFE PLAN is to:

Make an impressive, attitude changing, impact on your life by seriously considering what it is you really want.

Why you want it.

How badly you want it.

Producing an exciting and credible overview of your life.

The purpose and object of your future

Establishing what the desired outcome is for every area of your life

Understanding the power of WHY? WHAT? WHEN? HOW?

WHY do you want to change your life?
WHY do you want more than you have?
WHY do you think you are entitled to more?
WHY do you think you haven't got it now?

WHAT is it you want
WHAT is it you already have that you want rid of?
WHAT are you prepared to do to get what you want?
WHAT have you done in the past?

WHEN do you need to realise this dream
WHEN do you need to escape your present circumstances
WHEN did you decide to do something about it
WHEN did you last really try?

HOW can you achieve more than you have done in the past?
HOW can you undo the damage that has already been done?
HOW can you be sure of success?
HOW much effort are you prepared to put in the achievement?

If any of these questions touch a nerve or ring a bell then you will be experiencing the first exciting tingle of recognition that the principal function of your body is to carry your head and within that head is one awesome piece of equipment.

The WHY, WHAT, WHEN and HOW techniques will help you programme the 'headtop' computer and fuel your ascendance up to where you think you belong.

Make a list of the people you have been sufficiently impressed with throughout your life from childhood to have effected your decisions. and then write down why you were impressed with them.

What your list might look like

Name	Why they impressed me

Now consider the decisions you made – based on the advice or example of these bench models you have elected.

Perhaps you have been impressed by someone's' physical appearance or their sense of humour. Perhaps their reputation or their position has impressed you.

The important revelation from making the list is to recognise whether that person had any credibility in areas other than those you were impressed with.

Thousands of little boys are impressed by the footballing skills of someone who is idolised by millions, including their father and elder brothers, but the important factor is that they can separate and even isolate the adulation from other aspects of, an otherwise low achiever, who just happens to be a talented football player.

I was always impressed by my parents and both of them would always feature right at the top of my list but, when I am forced to consider why, it becomes apparent to me that the reasons are all emotional. My father was virtually uneducated yet was my principal advisor when I was making decisions about higher education. He had my welfare at heart but had no personal experience and was possibly a major factor in my academic failure.

This is a reason, not an excuse, and when you start to understand the reasons why you made the wrong decision or why you failed in the past it helps you realise also that, if you had made the correct frames of referral, some of your failures might never have occurred. If you get my drift here you will then realise the power of the information gained from WHY LISTS.

You can make up a WHY LIST about virtually anything and, if you are honest with yourself, get down to the real reasons why something went wrong, why something failed or why you feel inadequate. Once you tag it and admit that it was a bad decision, the wrong advice or whatever then you are prepared to concede that it just might be possible to achieve something more in the future.

Having taken some time to re-evaluate your present circumstances you could be looking at a variety of reactions.

You could be feeling that things are much better than you realised and that possibly you should be grateful for what you have and where you are and you should be more appreciative of those who share your life.

If this is the case then you most definitely want to work on your PERSONAL PLAN to enhance your input, improve your disposition and stabilise what you have now come to recognise as being what you want.

If you are now rejoicing in the awareness of some latent ability and feel the excitement of recognising your potential then you should be itching to get into this PLAN and the first thing to dwell on is the CHANGE FACTOR. Remember the formula for change.

$$C = D + V + FS + E + NS$$

Nobody changes if they are comfortable and the thing that will make you instantly uncomfortable with what you have is the realisation of what you could have.

WHAT?

Does age effect your chance of success?

Does academic background effect your chance of success?

Does background and personal history effect your chance of success?

WHEN?

Establishing the reality of life with each individual you have a relationship

Preparing a Life Plan which will effectively lead to achievement

How ?

The essential core skills for success:

Attitude control

Communication Ability

Problem Solving

Time Management

Motivation

Visualisation

Lateral Thinking

Goal Setting

Perception

Decision Making

1876 - As to Bell's talking telephone, it only creates interest
in scientific circles - The commercial values will be
extremely limited.

Elisha Gray

When?

Planning requires time targets and mile stones and these can only be realistically established after careful research and analyses.

To set unrealistic victory lines, (I refuse to use the term Deadline on the basis that I will not put extra effort into anything that leads to Dead - Victory and the Winning Line are much more inspirational), will only lead to unfulfilled expectations, disillusionment and probable failure or even abondonment of your project.

Never be impressed by anothers persons' time scale because they are performing on a different stage and with a different script. Only you know your full set of personal circumstances and, to understand your ability inside a time ratio you have to establish the reality of who you are and where you are:

Basic Planning

Appreciating yourself

To see yourself as others see you but never deny the evidence of the reflection

What are you good at (*Strengths*)?

What are your limitations (*Weaknesses*)

What advantages do you have ?

Setting a time scale (*Time Management*)

Setting standards

Enlisting help (*Networking*)

Now you know what you want and how far you are from your target. You know what it takes and how long you have to achieve it. It is time to learn the skills and start the action.

> *1959 - I give Castro a year. No longer*
>
> President Fulgencio Batista

How?

Skills: *Mindstorming*

To establish a desired outcome over a measured period of time
Develop an understanding of Parallel /Overlapping Goals i e Social goals and Career ambitions should be supportive of each other and not conflicting:

Making Decisions

Analysing situations

> *1974 - It will be many years, and certainly not in my life,*
> *before the Tory party has a female leader and Britain has a*
> *woman as Prime Minister*
>
> Margaret Thatcher

Choice

Choice is another new world dictionary word.

The choice of degree of personal development is yours. You can choose to be nothing or to do nothing, but if you do you must be prepared to accept that you are also likely to have nothing if others choose not to contribute to or support your lifestyle. That is their right.

You can choose to be nothing but, in doing so, you choose to forego your control factors and that means that the government, at any point in time, may decide to abolish your right to welfare or your parents may decide to rent out your room. You have no control over your lifestyle.

In this changing world those who have the most sought after skills, the most applicable attitude, the ability to communicate, the vision and the application are the most likely to gain the power and the control.

Personal Development builds independence of others

Personal Development creates inner strength, belief and control

Personal Development excludes external pressures.

Personal Development means:

Developing yourself into everything you are capable of being.

CRITERION

I hereby release myself from the restrictions of self limiting beliefs.

I give myself the right to be me and to function as I choose.

I undertake to be true to myself, and accept full responsibility and accountability for my own life as I seek to achieve fulfilment of my needs and goals.

I desire the freedom to choose for myself

With complete freedom of choice I have decided to be:

> I recognise that the purpose of my life is to maximise the potential I have been given at birth and I choose to treat myself with respect and dignity and advance towards fulfilment in love and maximise my wisdom, freedom and joy knowing that I am the ultimate authority over me.

I choose to be me

To be everything I am capable of being

I..choose to be **free**

Want to try another Evaluation?

Do you understand the intended purpose of what you have read so far?

- Was the purpose achieved?
- Was the message relevant to you?
- Can you use this information?
- Will you use this information?
- How will you use this information?
- Where and when will you use it?

Dependent on how far down that list you answered positively you should now choose from:

- Progress to the next stage
- Read the previous chapter again
- Try macramé

A diet is a period of starvation
followed by a sharp weight increase
Never eat anything that walks out of the fridge
Never eat anything heavier than yourself

People who never read are no better off than
people who cannot read

Required Reading

I WAS ENCOURAGED to write this book by the many people who have informed me they derived benefit from my workshops and talks. In doing so I realised I could reach a much wider audience and help many more people realise their dreams. I set myself the goal to complete the book in one month. Often I regretted that goal because I was tired and my heavy work schedule demanded I should sleep, but I kept thinking, 'Somewhere out there another person may be writing a similar book and they also may be getting tired. If I just write for another hour I will get my book on the shelf before they do.' I finished the book in ten months. If I hadn't set the goal for one month it would have taken me ten years.

Now you have had the opportunity to share my experiences in life and applied my perceptions, theories and philosophies to your life and to your immediate circumstances, perhaps you will feel you haven't done so bad after all and you will be self satisfied and feeling sorry for those, like me, who believe they have seen the light.

If this is the case and you are now feeling really good about your own abilities and actually developing thoughts of superiority, do remember the purpose of the book is to make you think positively, recognise your potential and believe in yourself.

It has obviously worked 100% for you.

If you are not some arrogant egomaniac and the book has in any way stimulated your self belief or your desire to aim a little higher in some area of your life, then I congratulate you on reaching the crucial stage in maximising your potential.

You obviously wanted to increase your potential when you bought this book and you sustained interest to reach this stage. If you intend taking positive action as a result of reading this book, then you are aware of the very real possibility of enhancing your chances.

Here is your reward !

The book is unfinished because this is where I entrust you to personalise it and complete the last chapter which is really a whole new book. Your book. The book of the story, starting from where you are now and how you got there and everything that you did to get to where you want to be and how you got everything you want to have and became everything you want to become.

Only you can do this because only you know what you want and only you know how badly you want it and how much you are prepared to pay in effort, time and mental isolation to get it.

I have encouraged you to do various focus exercises throughout my book and now I have outlined a structure for this final section. Use all of the information you have amassed about yourself to good advantage, set your plan and get everything you want from life!

At this stage it is perfectly reasonable to accept that you cannot be expected to be all things and to know everything that is necessary for the success of your plan but it is more than likely that you will know someone who does have the information or the contact you require and, if they don't, they will know who does.

Who do you know who knows someone who knows someone who knows what you need to know?

Networking – Personal/Professional

Start right now compiling your list of contacts and, as you make your list, consider what you might have to negotiate with. You would be surprised how many meaningful favours I have seen performed by people in powerful positions in return for little more than courtesy.

CHAPTER ONE

Your Book

CHAPTER ONE should be your perception of your own self assessment. It should give a clear picture of who you are and what you are. Where you are and why you are where you are and what you do where you are.

Chapter One of Your Book should be as the first chapter in a book you have read for the first time. You must write it as though the reader knows nothing atall about you or your personal history but, for the purpose of understanding the ensuing story, it is essential that the reader knows your every thought and your reason for thinking. You are the reader and you are the most interesting person in the world – *to you*!

Your Book

THE FINAL CHAPTER should be your desired outcomes, your dreams, fantasies and life targets. It should be well documented in time and great detail – Just as you visualise the perfect ending to your plans. This must be written immediately after the first chapter to develop a beginning and an end. The intervening chapters will be your development plan. The story of how you made the transition told in advance. That is a plan and if you structure it with quality research and in depth personal analyses, you will come to believe in it and you will expect it to happen and, in this life, we usually get what we expect because we prepare for it.

Your Book

THESE CHAPTERS are the story of your personal development plan. They contain detail upon detail of each small step with time references, support, research and analyses. They are advance records of your perceived and potential challenges and how you overcame them and your emotional reaction to controlled success.

Glossary

PYO Something which awakens basic and barbaric thoughts invariably directed at an AH. If no action is taken to counteract or remove some thing you perceive as a PYO it can lead to many unpleasant conditions such as chronic irritable bowel syndrome, alcoholic dependence, arson, assassination or regular viewing of Coronation Street.

PMO Someone who tells me they got nothing out of reading this book.

FIFO The basic concept of good, old fashioned, team spirit.
Fit in or make other arrangements

SBS Also known in business circles as a SUIT. Someone who complies with the expected behaviour pattern.

Genuine SBSs are totally incapable of originating any thing. They comply with the rule book to the letter and are seen by institution as safe and predictable and therefore often rise to positions well above their ability, resulting in facial expressions which match their hair style.

The dedicated and active MP often impersonates an SBS to overcome some social prejudice and oil the wheels of commercial negotiation. This disguise may fool some of the people all of the time and fool all of the people some of the time but lubrication will release the shaggy dog and expose the happy chappie that lives within the suit like a hermit crab unlike the real SBS who bears more resemblance to a dung beetle.

LEP This is a person who conducts a personal campaign against charity shops, brew their own beer partly to curtail the cost of drinking and partly to enhance the production of methane as a free source of energy. They spend their entire life capturing and containing and perfecting the art of recycling until they eventually disappear up heir own theories.

MP Motivated Person or Member of Parliament. Seldom both!

PM Porridge Making.